Pocketbook of Presentation Excellence

Tips and best practice to speak confidently in any business situation from a veteran Professional Speaker

Paul Archer

High House Publishing

First published in Great Britain in 2017 by High House Publishing, High House, Priors Norton, Gloucestershire, GL2 9LS, United Kingdom.

Printed and bound in Great Britain by Lulu.com.

Copy edited by Angie Bruce

Cover designed by Vector Designs

ISBN 978-0-9933112-8-4 (Paperback)

ISBN 978-0-9933112-9-1 (eBook)

For all your sales coaching needs and in-house requirements, contact Paul at:

paul@paularcher.com
www.paularcher.com
www.presentation-excellence.co.uk

This book is dedicated not to an individual, but to all members of the Professional Speaking Association here in the UK who I've watched, networked with and learnt from since 2000 and to all the audiences I've presented to since my first presentation in 1989.

Table of Contents

Introduction

As a successful speaker and trainer, I really wanted to put pen to paper to record my speaking experiences over the last twenty years.

I wanted to do this because I wish for others to gain immediately from what I've learned since I began to speak and train for a living in 1990.

It's a cliché that we learn by experience, making mistakes and learning from these, getting valuable feedback from others and observing and learning from the very best in the job.

But it's true. This book could knock a few years off your development cycle.

Please enjoy and let me know what value it brings to you.

Tips to Harness Your Nerves

Why Nerves are Good

Imagine your audience are all sitting on the toilet. That advice only made me giggle so I couldn't use that. Then I was shown the image of butterflies flying all around your stomach and was told to make sure these butterflies flew in formation, and this was to banish my nerves. This told me the theory, but not how to handle my nerves. Next, I was told to imagine my audience were stark naked and this had a similar result to the toilet.

Finally, someone gave me some solid advice - rename nerves and call it adrenaline. The advice went on to say that you'll never get rid of them; so use them to your advantage, since you need adrenaline to do a good job. When I was told this many moons ago, it finally began to put it all into context.

Now if you want to feel nervous, just imagine you are standing at the front of a landing craft just about to ditch on the Normandy beaches in June 1944. Now that, I can imagine, would be nerve racking. I remember the film, Saving Private Ryan, when the US forces were being sick with fear ready to face certain death.

Now I know where I would rather be, and I think you'll agree, standing up in front of people compares very favourably with the Normandy Landings.

But you will get nerves or adrenaline flushes before presenting. If you don't, then stop speaking in public because you don't care anymore. You need adrenaline as this makes you do your utmost best. Controlling this natural energy is vital. Apart from adopting the right body posture, and using your arms to gesture freely, I want to give you 4 further ways of handling the adrenaline to your advantage. In no particular order, I'll give you peripheral vision, lubricating your voice box, taking a slurp, and visualisation.

Go Peripheral Vision

Peripheral vision was taught to me a few years ago. Now, I've always struggled to have a wide peripheral vision apparently because I'm a man. Women have naturally more powerful peripheral vision and that's just because women's brains are wired differently. My mum always had eyes in the back of her head, and Alan Pease's excellent book, Why Women Can't Read Maps… shows you this.

So what does this have to do with adrenaline control? Well, imagine you're up on your stage and feeling a little anxious and energetic. Maybe you're being introduced or you have a natural moment to pause. Focus on a point in front of you and stretch your peripheral vision right down to your ears and imagine these are your extra eyes.

Do this for a few seconds and you will be instantly relaxed. How? The brain is wired so that you cannot consciously process nerves and peripheral vision simultaneously. Clever isn't it? Try it next time, it really does work.

Lubricate Your Mouth

As a speaker, your voice is by far the most important asset, only second to your body. By the way, PowerPoint comes down very low in priority. Your voice is the vehicle in which the message is given to your audience, so make sure it is ready and willing. What can you do if your mouth is drying up, and the water is miles away from where you're standing?

If you have slightly less than a minute available to you, tear a tiny piece of paper millimetres in size, and fold it into a tiny ball. Wedge this in the back of your mouth behind your teeth, so you don't swallow. Make sure no one can see you doing this, otherwise they'll think you're taking performance enhancing drugs, and we don't want that now do we?

Your mouth now thinks there's something in there and will automatically produce saliva. And that's what you want - to lubricate your mouth at that vital moment. Try it, but do practise first, it does work.

Taking a Slurp

On the subject of dry mouths, the next tip was given to me about 10 years ago by a chap called Frank. Frank was from the East End of London and had a wonderful gritty accent. Now when Frank got lost or wanted to check his notes, he would call out to the audience that he wanted a "slurp".

Off he went to the side of the room where he kept his bottle of water and glass. He would make a song and dance over opening the bottle - fizzy was best. It made a loud 'psst' when it was opened, and he poured the water vigorously into his glass and took a couple of big slugs. All of this was done very dramatically and, sure enough, many of the audience would copy him if they had water in front of them.

Meanwhile Frank could have a good look at his notes to see where he was and to settle down any nerves he might have had. Very clever.

Whilst on the subject of notes, you should have them. Not a script of your speech but something containing bullets or reminders of what to say next. Now Frank would never hold onto his notes as that stilted his body language and use of gestures. Take care with using PowerPoint as your notes;

many people do it. If you do this you'll end up having a slide for every single part of your presentation since they are your notes. You'll end up being accused of "Death by PowerPoint" and nobody wants that.

Do you?

Visualise for Success

My final tip for you to overcome your nerves or ensure they're channelled to assist you, not hinder you, is major dollops of visualisation. Now this is not new at all and many sport stars use this to increase their success.

Do you recall the 2003 Rugby World Cup final a fair few years ago, when Jonny Wilkinson scored all those points? I was told recently by someone in the know what Jonny does to ensure success and to channel his nerves. The hand clasping routine, and the moments of pure concentration before he heads off into his run were his way of imagining the ball being kicked and flying into the air, clearing the sticks to score 3 valuable points - before it even happened.

Mohammed Ali was perhaps the greatest champion of visualisation. He called it Future History and would predict the result of all his fights. And he got it right many more times than he got it wrong. "Ashley Moore, I'll have you down in four." And he did.

You see the way the brain is wired ensures that if you visualise and imagine an event in your head and if you do this strongly enough, I mean really intensely; colour, movement, panoramic views, sounds, people, laughter and you're part of it, then the brain will eventually believe it to be true.

So next time you have a big speech coming up, play a movie in your head of it all going very well indeed, maybe even a standing ovation. Go on; really pump up the success in the movie. Only you know it's there.

So there we have 4 quick little tips to use the next time you have an important meeting to speak at. Apart from plenty of preparation and practice, and let's face it, we have loads of time for this, use your peripheral vision, lubricate your mouth, take a slurp and visualise your success.

It's nothing really new probably, but then again the best tips are always the oldest. They were given to me by experienced presenters and I'm now passing them onto you.

Relax More to Perform

Great stand-up comedians are relaxed, inspiring speakers are relaxed, moving salespeople are relaxed.

When you're relaxed, you can perform effortlessly, you can ad lib as the situation requires, you feel confident, you come across as self-assured.

It's an obvious notion, but the secret is to relax, but how? Here are some ideas:

- Visualise success happening in the event that's coming up. Perhaps a standing ovation if you're a speaker.
- Learn to breathe fully; how is another article. Most of us breathe to survive, not to thrive in the pressure cooker situation we find ourselves in. Breathing in deeper and then breathing out slower is the key to effective breathing.
- Curb the extremities. Watch the hands and the feet – if you are feeling slightly apprehensive, then this will show in your feet and hands moving uncontrollably.

- Spot the motivational zone that you're in. Move away from "need" from "drive" and get "in the zone". Only from there are you truly relaxed and on form.
- Practise a positive mental attitude. PMA is well known but if you think positive thoughts and rid yourself of negative past thinking, then you'll enter a positive relaxed mode.
- Believe in yourself and your ability; you know you can provide massive value to your customers.
- Learn to contain the inner critic in us all. Realise you can't get rid of him altogether, just silence or mute him with effort. Pen him in.
- Practise whatever you do regularly.
- Handle feedback well. Yes, receive it graciously, but if you don't believe in it or didn't seek it from that person, then drop it. Not in an arrogant way please, but if it's provided when you didn't ask for it, or you don't agree, drop it.
- Learn to relax more, enjoy your job and give value.

Presenter State

"I don't like your attitude" shouted my fifth grade teacher as I was evicted from the class. Schooling for me only improved from my disruptive early period. Having the right attitude can influence many a speaker as can having the wrong one.

The right state of mind is crucial to an effective presentation and you owe it to your audience to get into the right state. Here's how.

Remove all Concerns

Remove all concerns from your head. We've all baggage of some sorts in our head. A lingering argument with your partner, a major mistake you made yesterday or the loss of a deal can all affect your state of mind. The trick is to adopt mindfulness and empty the head so you can focus on the now. A favourite Dandy Warhols' number from the early noughties talks about having a trap door in the back of my head. I use this metaphor to empty out all the thoughts that are bringing me down before I perform on the stage. It works.

Music

On the subject of the Dandy Warhols, let's get into music and the effect it can have on your state of mind. As I write this, I'm listening to my State Changer Playlist on my phone. This playlist consists of a number of songs, tunes and tracks from my collection that each control and influence my state of mind. I'm 33,000 feet above the Himalayas having presented in Bangladesh and I just fancied a boost of energy, so I'm listening to my playlist.

Music is an anchor. The listening can bring back a state of mind which you either experienced when you listened to the track or you embedded into the tune at a later date. Anchors do this. Anchors can be any sense – hearing something, seeing an image in your head, a physical touch on your body, a smell or a taste. They all relive a state of mind for you.

Collect anchors for each and every state you need. I use my playlist as it has an instant state changing capability and I love my tunes. Right now I'm listening to "I am the Resurrection" from the Stone Roses, voted the number 10 guitar tune by Q Magazine. It revs me up so I can go out into the audience and "give 'em large".

Among my playlist I've:

- *The Raven* by The Stranglers for extra energy
- *Good Morning Britain* by Aztec Camera for inspiration
- *One Day Like This* by Elbow for concentration
- *Nothing in My Way* by Keane for perseverance
- *Glory Days* by Pulp for stimulation

You may see it differently.

Physical Comfort

In 2016 I attended a private medical since I was applying for some additional medical insurance. The doctor knew his stuff and half way through stated to me with no emotion or prejudice, "Lose a stone". I shed 25 pounds that year, continued going to the gym but started doing weights and toned up a little. Boy did it make a difference to how I felt when presenting. It meant all my clothing was a whole lot looser and felt so much more comfortable.

Being physically comfortable is essential. Loose clothing helps, but learn to stand well; I call it the assertive stance. Ensure your body is perfectly balanced, no leaning on either leg, legs the same width as your shoulders, slightly apart. Girls, get rid of your finishing school poses. Balanced, posture upright, shoulders back – just like your mum told you before you disembarked for school.

Breathing

Breathe to thrive not just survive, was a phrase I heard at the annual convention of the Professional Speaking Association. Breathing is more than just surviving; it can affect your state of mind. Let me continue the story of my private doctor from earlier.

He asked me to lie on the couch and he progressed to measure my blood pressure. I have to confess to being a little nervous at the time, you see deep down I'm a big baby. After his first measure, he instructed me to calm down having stated there's no way he could submit that blood pressure to the insurance company, as they'd reject my application.

I thought, how can I relax? Breathing I recalled. Breathe in deeply and breathe out very slowly, verrry slowly. I did this for one minute and he measured my blood pressure again. "That's better, much more normal".

I breathed a sigh of relief.

So if you are a little nervous, and your blood pressure is rising, do the breathing technique before you go on stage for a couple of minutes. It will calm you down, lower your heart rate and put you in a more relaxed state of mind – a presenter's state.

Take in the Room

The aim here is to become one with the group. You will do that as your talk proceeds but to gain the right state at the beginning, adapt to peripheral vision. Many presenters will use their foveal vision and focus on a particular spot; this has no value to become one with the room. Instead pick a spot but deliberately enhance your peripheral capability by concentrating on everything around you. This trains your brain to use peripheral vision as you begin your talk, thus taking in the whole audience.

Usually somebody introduces me on the stage – this takes 20 seconds or so. I typically stand to the side behind the introducer, ready to pounce but as she introduces me, I focus on her but let my peripheral vision do its magic by taking in the whole room and every member of the audience that I can.

As I begin my talk, my brain is in peripheral mode and this lets me become one with them. I then relax the peripheral and go foveal, ensuring I give as many people eye contact as I can. The eyes are the windows to the soul, let's never forget that.

Gain Control of the Room

The bigger the audience, the bigger the applause you'll get after the introduction and the more effort you'll want to exert to gain control. Here's how:

1. Peripheral into foveal eye contact around the room.
2. Breathe and adopt the assertive stance, be balanced and relaxed.
3. The audience will now also relax.
4. Present.

A clip round the ear from the headmaster soon cured my attitude all those years ago. Hey, you can't do that anymore, can you? Or the cane, which I endured twice. Hasn't the world changed but presenting to an audience will always require that you have the right state of mind.

Planning Your Presentation

Perfect Presentation Planning

In my "in tray" right now is a letter from my accountant, wanting me to fill in some forms, and make some journal adjustments to my Sage Instant Accounts program. The forms are heavy - very heavy - and to be quite honest with you, I keep putting it off.

They call that 'procrastination', but I'm really not looking forward to doing it.

In business, you often have to make presentations to groups of people. The problem is, you may not do presentations regularly, and the thought of preparing might give you the same reaction as my tax forms.

Come on, hands up. Who's guilty of going to PowerPoint immediately you need to do a presentation? If so, then my template might be able to save you time preparing, and help you to put together a first class presentation that will get fantastic results.

The template is in the form of a triangle and deliberately so.

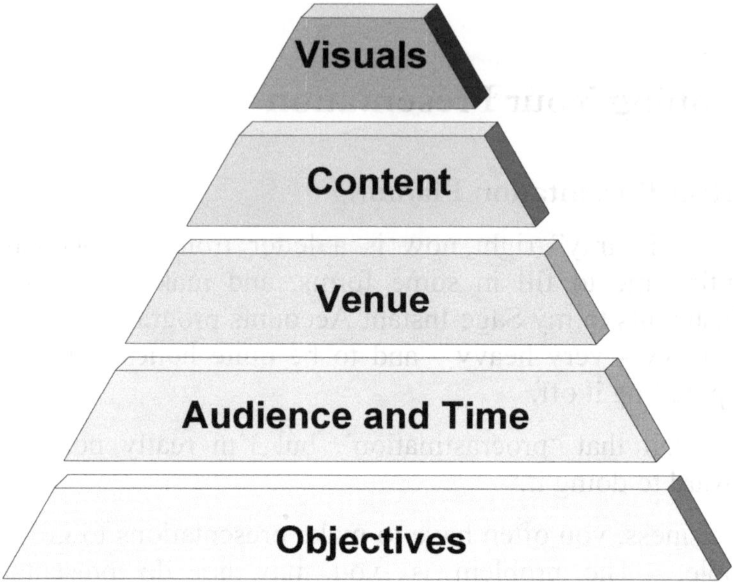

Objectives

We're having an extension built on our home at the moment. It's being built above our existing single storey kitchen. The local building regulations inspector wanted to check that the existing foundations were sufficient to support two stories and we had to dig a bore hole first.

In the same way, a business presentation, in fact any presentation will fall down without the right foundations and these foundations are the objectives. They give purpose and direction for your speech and allow you to measure success. In today's world, measuring all activity is a must.

You've probably heard of SMART objectives, which is a very useful acronym on how to structure any business objective, but what I want you to do is to switch the focus. Away from you and to your audience, who are actually more important than you. It's not what you want to achieve…it's what the audience want to get out of listening to you talk.

My experience has shown that business presentation audiences want to do one of three things. As a result of listening to you, they want to:

1. Be able to do something, or
2. Understand something, or
3. Agree to do something.

Naturally your talk might want to help them attain a few of these objectives but you do have to be very careful in not trying to achieve too much. The last objective, agree to do something, might only happen if the earlier objective of understanding is achieved and it's highly unlikely you'll get the whole audience to commit to do something. Typically one or two key decision makers might be your target rather than the entire audience, unless you speak like Winston Churchill or Adolf Hitler.

Audience and Time

If there's one message that you take away from this chapter, and let's be honest, that's usually the way with many things we read, it's that the audience is king, and should be put up there on the throne. How much time do we spend researching our audience:

- Who they are?
- Why are they attending?
- What time of day is it going to be?
- What knowledge do they already have?

- What attitudes and beliefs do they have?
- How many of them are there?
- What's their background?

And so on. Really focus on your audience. I remember vividly the time I blew it with the audience. I was to deliver a presentation to some managers on how to appraise their staff. Standard content I thought and as the request was from someone via someone else through another person, I took along my standard presentation.

What a mistake. The managers worked for an engineering company that made pumps. They were engineers, I mean real engineers; into structure, process, logic, arguments, testing, trade unions and so on. They were smashing guys but a very different audience to whom I would normally address. That was my mistake for not finding out beforehand.

Let me show you something really clever that I picked up a few years back, in fact, following my engineer goof. Imagine a three legged stool in your kitchen. Each leg is quite the same as the next – they are all in balance and the stool stands perfectly on the floor. Now if someone came along with a stool with one leg shorter that the other, the stool would soon fall over especially if I tried to sit on it.

In business presentations your three legs of the stool stand for objectives, time and audience and they all need to be in balance for the stool to stand up. If one is out of line, then the stool (your presentation) will fall over.

Let me give you an example. If someone else fixes the audience, the time and the objective, you're usually on a hiding for nothing. Some years ago I was asked by a sales director to address his entire sales team on how to negotiate client fees effectively. The venue was a smart hotel and the event was their annual sales conference.

The audience numbered over 100 and the time I was allowed was 30 minutes, and that was assuming the person before me didn't over-run (and they always do). Now this was impossible to achieve in 30 minutes and if I went ahead as requested I would have bombed. Instead, thankfully, we negotiated the objective and dumbed it right down. We also arranged for further workshops to address the remaining objectives with fewer than 12 people per workshop.

The stool needs to be balanced and aligned, otherwise you might bomb.

Venue

Often overlooked in our preparation, is the actual venue you'll be speaking at. Now it might be the company's board room which you've used dozens of times before, but it might be a local hotel for example, which you don't know about. The golden rule is to own the venue yourself, not nip out and buy it, but become very close to it. If your presentation is important enough, visit the venue to assess where the screen will be, where you'll sit, the air conditioning, windows, the microphone etc.

Here's another tip if you have to present to an audience around a traditional board room table. You know the type – enormous and too heavy to even contemplate moving and often highly polished. Big comfy chairs too. The worst thing is that the screen is right at the front of the table where you are supposed to present from.

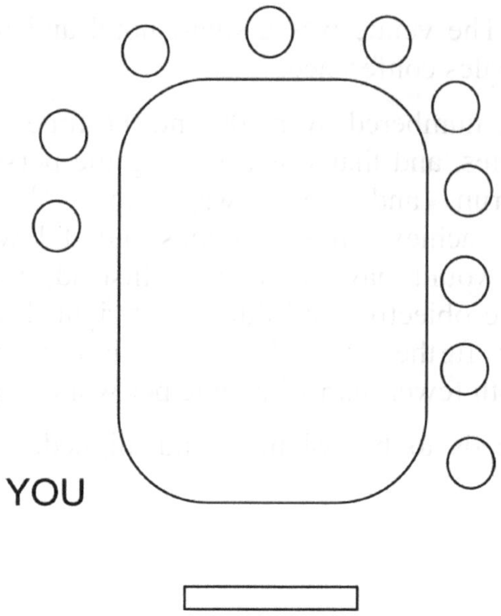

The trick here is to remove the chairs in the bottom left hand part of the table and make the whole corner your delivery zone. The screen can stay where it is and because you've moved some chairs where your delivery corner is, the whole audience can see you and the screen.

If you're using PowerPoint to add to your delivery, check out the lighting in the room. Earlier this year I had to deliver a presentation in a hotel conservatory. The natural daylight was wonderful but completely drowned out my slides. I had to go to plan B and use the flipchart instead.

Content

At long last, I hear you shout; the actual content of the presentation. The most common mistake that we all do is put too much content into our presentations. We can bombard our audience with just too much to take in one swallow.

Now there are ways of making your message stand out for the audience so they remember more, but that's the subject of another book. In the meantime, copy what the professionals do, which is to limit the number of points you want to make. Aristotle once said that presentations are easy – you make your point and then back it up. Use arguments, stats, stories, anecdotes, participation, quotes, graphics and pictures. It's what the pro's do; they make a point and then support it.

You know this new Sky Plus that's being heavily promoted at the moment? One of the key features is that if the phone rings or you need a toilet break, you can pause the live TV show and return to exactly where you left off whilst the rest of the country are watching the same show a few minutes ahead of you. Useful I imagine.

In presentations, people don't physically go to the toilet (although some do) or answer the phone (although some still do) but they do lose attention sometimes and wander somewhere else in their mind. That's why you should continually loop back to earlier points by providing summaries and reminders to help people get the message.

Here's a useful template that I use when designing the content for a 30 to 40 minute presentation:

What	Time	Why	How
Opening Bang and hook your audience			
Point 1			
Point 2			
Point 3			
Summary			
Questions			
Closing Bang			

Allocating time is useful to keep you on track. Asking yourself why helps you to bridge the content over to your audience. Why do they want to know the point, what's in it for them? The how, is the method of delivery you'll use. Will it be talk, an audience exercise, a story told, a visual aid, a video?

Try not to fall into the trap of always delivering it the same old way because that's the way you've always done it. I was guilty of this a few years ago. I would always roll out the slides and when projectors arrived it was even easier for me to roll out even more slides, with all the bells and whistles I could muster. A big mistake that took me a long time to realise.

A B2B Sales Presentation Structure

It's about them, not you. The last thing a sales presentation needs is information about you. I've seen countless sales presentations with the ubiquitous "about us" slides, created by marketing and delivered by sales.

Boring, irrelevant and essentially selfish.

It's about the customer. Here's how you do it:

Challenges

The first part of the sales presentation must highlight the challenges or issues the customer is experiencing to enable you to provide your solution. For every sale there are always issues. The aim here is to encourage your customers in the audience to start nodding their heads and realise that you've understood their challenges that brought you here.

Introduce yourself, of course, but do it verbally. You do not want a slide for this.

Key Insights

This is your chance to reveal any juicy information and insights you've gained as part of your research. Any perceptions that you can reveal here will demonstrate to your customer that you have a handle on this and have thought it through.

Implications

Continuing your insights into their challenges, here you reveal any implications of the challenges continuing and festering.

What's the impact, where will it take the client, where will this lead? Not only is this your opportunity to determine that you really understand the client's situation and influences, but you will also show that the solution you'll be revealing shortly has been well thought through.

Story

Now comes the story. Everyone likes a short story. This could be an existing customer who struggled with the same challenge. Describe insights and issues. Stories should be: context, challenge, journey, solution.

Shape of Solution

Now comes your solution. Keep it flexible so you give the impression that it's not a "done deal" and can be improved and adapted by you and the customer. The solution must show how the challenge can be overcome and the results for the customer.

Why us?

Now comes the proof piece. Why now and not earlier? Research shows that as soon as a customer hears a solution, their first reaction will be proof and risk. If you are to deliver the solution, what proof do you have, and what experience do you have in this area? Remember, a customer's knee jerk reaction is to stick with the status quo. If they are to move forward they will need to eliminate any fear of risk or loss.

Proving why you can offer the solution is essential at this juncture.

Call to Action

The classic close: The call to action. Ask the customer how he wants to move forward or suggest the next step to the sale in your sales process.

Keep to this structure and you won't go far wrong. And if the marketing department insists on you delivering their standard deck, politely refuse.

2 Rashers Please

"Two rashers please" asked the elderly hotel guest as Mr Rana took her order for breakfast.

Mr Rana runs a delightful hotel in Gidea Park where I was staying on business. His hotel is spotlessly clean, has off-street parking and 60 megabyte broadband. And he serves up a delicious breakfast. He's been over here for over 20 years and speaks perfect English.

But the *"two rashers"* stumped him.

Having no idea what she meant, the lady quickly repeated, *"Two rashers of bacon please"*.

Rashers is colloquial English, almost jargon, and we all use it.

Last month I was working with some Generation Ys about their sales skills and I said they might be able to earn a bob or two more with these new skills. They looked dumbfounded so I asked them quizzically, *"What does that mean to you?"* A haircut, they replied.

Of course a bob hasn't represented a shilling since 1971, I think, so how would they know what I meant?

We all use jargon without even knowing. If it's used internally in your company or industry and you're talking to industry people, then use it, as it accelerates communication.

I hope you're completing your structured CPD as a result of your SPS from the CII?

Certain people would understand that.

But when addressing customers, spot when you're doing it and stop it. Simple really and we already know this.

Just as I knew that waiting for Mr Rana's rashers is well worth the delay; they're the best in Romford.

Conciseness is the Future

"I didn't have time to prepare a long speech" - Churchill

When presenting at sale meetings or board room presenting, it's good to be concise – time is the key element. Here are some ideas to be more concise.

- 30 seconds answer maximum to all questions at the Q&A.
- Be concise when introducing yourself – keep it to 30 seconds.
- When presenting information, learn to pause and stop waffling, just bite your tongue.
- Stop earlier in sentences than you normally would.
- If they want more information, they'll ask.
- Keep information to one page,

- Keep slides to a minimum. Google *Pecha Kucha* if you want to try something quicker and punchier with PowerPoint - http://www.pechakucha.org/
- If they're quiet it means they've got it, so move on to your next topic.

The Jinx of Too Much Knowledge

"As you are all aware…"

Well I wasn't but I was too embarrassed to say anything and within a minute the presenter had lost me. I had no idea what he was talking about, yet he promised to make things crystal clear.

I was with a new client this week who was steeped in their way of doing things and the technical terms surrounding their operations. Their first conversation went straight over my head with all the technical jargon used. I needed to understand, so I pleaded with them to explain in layman's terms, which they did.

It is a curse, a jinx, a major communication blunder when we know too much about a topic and assume that everyone else has a basic knowledge, so we can add to this.

The message for sales people and sales managers? If you are the subject matter expert, then good for you, but spend time working out how to explain the basics so that everyone can understand what you say. Here are some ideas:

- Use examples vigorously as these aid understanding.
- Break it down visually on a whiteboard.
- Go right back to basics.
- Check understanding with the group periodically.

- Find out your group's pre-knowledge of the topic.
- Try to simplify everything – it won't make you appear like a dunce – in fact it's quite the opposite. It takes intelligence to make something that is complex appear simple. It's far too easy to make something simple appear complex.

That's the problem with having too much knowledge.

How to Spice up Your Words

Ever listened to a really good presenter who just seemed to have the audience totally hypnotised with their every word? I'm sure you have. And I bet you've tried to copy them.

You see, these people don't do it by chance; they have carefully crafted their words to add more impact to their presentations.

And the good news is I'm going to share seven of these techniques with you. Even though words alone contribute little to the overall impact of communication, beef them up a little and you can make their input much more powerful.

Emphasis

With your words you can just say them or you can emphasise particular ones for an effect.

For example, say this sentence: "It is our best chance of success." Next say it by emphasising the "is" - "It is our best chance of success."

If you emphasise the word that may not normally be stressed, this produces even more impact.

Emphasis can also be produced by adding words that intensify the message. Have a listen to this:

- "We're doing well."
- "We're doing extremely well."

Now you could use the second sentence instead of the first, or use them both for even more oomph.

We can play around here even more by intensifying words to add impact to a statement:

- "We reject…" becomes "We totally reject…"
- "We regret…" becomes "We deeply regret…"
- "We encourage…" becomes "We positively encourage…"

Other words that can produce the same effect are:

- strongly
- freely
- sincerely
- enthusiastically
- utterly
- categorically
- fully
- honestly
- firmly
- readily

So play around with emphasis and don't be afraid of experimenting. Be afraid of the negative impact of dry monotone sentences. Be positively afraid.

Focusing

Focusing is a simple technique that uses the pattern "What…is…" in order to build anticipation in your audience.

Example:

- "I'd like to approach this question from two different angles."

becomes:

- "What I'd like to do is approach this question from two different angles."

Simple, yet very effective.

Repetition

You can use simple repetition to very, very good effect. Your speeches will then be much, much better and it will be far, far easier to grasp the importance of what you're saying.

An interesting variation on the theme of repetition is the following technique in which you make a statement, repeat it and then explain what you mean.

- "Nobody knows the answer to that one. Nobody!"

Other words you can use like this are:

- Always
- Ever
- Never

- Nothing

Rhetorical Questions

Rhetorical questions can be used as a device for engaging an audience and capturing their attention.

- "What do we all want? We want to shatter our targets this year, don't we all?"

Rhetorical questions can be used in the following way to good effect:

Statement + Rhetorical question + Answer

- "Let's turn to the question of being the number one performing department. What is our main objective? Our main objective is to…"

Dramatic Contrasts

Contrast is a common presentation technique that adds impact to a statement.

- Neil Armstrong: "That's one small step for man. One giant step for mankind."
- John F Kennedy: "Ask not what your country can do for you. Ask what you can do for your country."

Look at the following quotations and complete them. They all use contrast to good effect.

- Success is getting what you want. Happiness is…
- It's a recession when your neighbour loses his job. It's a depression when…
- Everything has been thought of before. The problem is to…

- If you owe your bank a hundred pounds, you have a problem. But if you owe it a million…
- I'd rather be a failure at something I enjoy than a success…

Tripling

Also known as the power of threes. A tried and tested technique is to chunk important points in threes.

Like this:

- Fast, efficient and friendly…
- Accessible, respectful and professional…
- Smart, enthusiastic and helpful etc…

Or like this:

- "What is a committee? A group of the unwilling, picked from the unfit to do the unnecessary."

Or like this:

- "I came, I saw, I conquered."

Machine-Gunning

Although three things are about as much as anyone can really take in, it is possible to add impact by using the machine-gunning effect. With this technique, the speaker reels off a list of six or seven points to impress the audience and persuade them with the force of their argument.

"The new model is faster, sleeker, smoother, classier, racier, roomier and better looking than anything else on the market!"

Such a phrase needs to be delivered at quite a fast pace, which accentuates the machine-gun effect.

Build-Ups

With this technique the speaker gives a number of bits of information which lead up to a short and simple conclusion or summary which says the same thing "in a nutshell".

For example:

"This new laptop has the most powerful processor, the fastest internet connection and the biggest screen on the market. In short, it is the best on the market!"

Knock-downs

This technique can add a touch of humour and provocation to a speech.

First, the speaker builds up a series of points and then finally knocks them all down with a single statement.

For example:

"They said DVD would never catch on, that it was too expensive for what it was, that nobody would be interested in the benefits, that the timing of it was all wrong... So, how come over 90% of the British population now own a DVD player?"

Nine pretty impressive techniques to make your words have that little extra impact.

Try one at a time to build up your confidence, but be careful you don't overdo each one as this can come over as cheesy and contrived. As my mum used to say to me about dieting...a little of everything is best.

What Makes a Talk and TED Talk

I was invited to give a 10 minute talk last month to an audience of 100 people. When asked how I was going to structure it, I said I'd do a TED style talk.

We've all heard of TED talks, watched them on YouTube and my client was intrigued to know more. "Paul I've seen and loved TED talks, but what specifically makes it a TED talk?"

So I answered:

1. A common theme throughout the talk.
2. Substance over style – it's the content that really matters, not necessarily the style.
3. 18 minutes max. Strip out detail, focus on the topic enough to be compelling; it's what you leave out that matters. The first draft of my talk lasted 15 minutes – too long, so instead of reducing the whole talk, I left out two or three key components, leaving the remainder compelling.
4. Have a structure that runs through the theme – settling down to start, the context of the issue, main issues and practical applications works well. Finish with a call to action.
5. Connect with the audience quickly – eye contact, humour, strip away your ego.
6. Lots of short stories and anecdotes.
7. Visuals work – no bullets or lists.
8. Memorise either the script or key points to remind you. Never use notes, never stand behind a lectern and read and never be tempted to use PowerPoint as your notes,

however professorial you are (if you want a quick way to memorise, which I always do – just email me).

9. Practise beforehand – run through from scratch – speed rehearse if you need to but never wing it, however experienced you are.
10. Have a compelling open – drama, ignite some curiosity, tease.
11. Finally the platform. Remove all barriers, nothing between your audience and you, make it natural as possible.

These are the ingredients of a TED talk. The preparation time is completely out of sync for the time to deliver – mine took days to prepare, memorise and practise. That's why TED talks are so cool.

Engaging the Audience

Presenting for Maximum Understanding

We all have to present information or an idea or a proposal and we aim to achieve maximum understanding of our message.

This is core to presenting, but how do we do it effectively?

My holiday to France this year is always a challenge when it comes to speaking to the French shopkeeper or passers-by. My French is basic O' Level stuff and my accent is non-existent, so I have to revert to other methods to get my message across. Sign language, using pictures or drawings, lots of smiles, sometimes slower, louder.

Here are 20 ways you can get your message across more effectively:

1. An analogy
2. A prop or an object to illustrate
3. An example
4. A quote
5. Some stats
6. A joke
7. A story or metaphor
8. A visual aid such as a diagram
9. A sound bite, song or tune
10. Summarising and repeating the message

11. An acronym or mnemonic
12. A question to elicit their understanding
13. A step by step guide
14. Humour
15. A demonstration
16. A YouTube video
17. A testimonial from a customer
18. A photograph
19. Acting out a scene
20. Showing them the real thing

I'm sure you can add some more, notice no PowerPoint.

So next time you need to get a point across, think of different more compelling ways to do so.

For our visit to France next year, I've been shown an app for my phone that will literally translate to French anything I speak into it in English. How cool is that? But it kinda destroys the whole fun of trying my hardest, making myself appear foolish and building a strong rapport because I'm trying my hardest to communicate. And in France there are only three words you need – du vin, du pain, du fromage.

Buckeroo and Attention Spans

I remember fondly on wet Sunday afternoons playing Buckeroo. You loaded up this spring mounted plastic horse with all sorts of plastic items – spades, boxes, blankets – the items got heavier and heavier and eventually the horse would bolt out of the springs, scaring you witless.

Great fun.

You see, there was only so many things the horse could carry before it bolted and that's a little like humans and their attention spans.

NLP says that we can only concentrate on around 7 things. We can only keep around 7 items in our head, in our conscious mind. Beyond that and we bolt like buckaroo.

We obviously don't bolt but if we are faced with handling more than 7 things, we ignore or our subconscious takes care of them. And that's where we can influence effectively. Let me explain some uses:

- Make sure when you're dealing with a customer or colleague that you want to influence, keep the distractions to a minimum. Apart from the obvious be aware of what's behind you, it's amazing what can distract. Remember 7.

- Deliberately overload the customer and then slip in some hypnotic influencing techniques. Here's a couple of them:
- Use the word "because" liberally to justify your reasons for your idea.
- Soften your voice and lower it for an influential tone.
- Match everything you can see and hear about your customer.

There's a whole list of things you can do whilst the customer is occupied and these serve to influence them. It's OK, it's only influencing.

Manchester United and the Big Picture

It was our first time going to Old Trafford even though I've supported my team since I was 7 years old. But our tickets were miles up in the north east stand and I said to my two boys that we're not going to able to see much, but at least there'll be a good atmosphere.

How wrong was I?

Because the stands are virtually vertical, we could see everything just by looking down at the pitch. I saw the defence positions when we were attacking. I saw the away fans in the corner making so much noise. I could see the linesmen running up and down the line and appreciated how complex their role is.

I had the whole scene in front of me. If I'd been watching on TV, yes I would've been closer to the play, but I would not know what was going on around the immediate vicinity of the ball and I would be at the behest of the cameraman.

In sales, we do need to have a firm eye on the bigger picture, especially if we want to cross or up sell. I prefer to call this upgrading – it's far more consumer friendly. By seeing the bigger picture, we can gauge the enormity of the problem the customer is struggling to solve, and see if there are other issues at play. Who makes the decisions? Who else is involved?

How do we do this? Like every aspect of selling, it's about the questions you ask.

- What's this a part of?
- What's the bigger picture behind this issue?
- What's the project that surrounds this?
- Is this part of a bigger issue?

I never knew that linesmen only run half a pitch. They only occupy one half each and work together to cover the pitch. I always wondered why they were so much quicker than the players.

Making the Complex Simple

It's the hardest thing to do but it's the sign of a true professional. Unfortunately the Bremain campaigners here in the UK have failed in this respect.

Let me explain.

David Cameron returned to the UK with a deal. Much fanfare occurred, Dave said, "We have the best of both worlds". The negotiations achieved have never appeared in their remain campaign because no one has cared to explain them. Here we go. The new deal:

1. Made it harder for Euro currency countries to dictate terms to non-Euro countries like Britain, Poland and Czechia.
2. Recognised that the EU will always have more than one currency.
3. Britain can block decisions made by Euro currency countries that we don't like.
4. Allows Britain to make their own rules when regulating financial services (our biggest export).

There, that wasn't so bad. We don't have to be told what to do all the time, we don't have to use the Euro and we won't need to bail anyone out. That wasn't too evil.

The lesson is to make complex information appear simple. Some ideas:

- Use infographics to show things visually. These can be bought for $5 if you outsource.
- Use cartoons or animations to explain something.

- Use simple words to explain things. It's not dumbing down, but a courtesy to your listener.

The Art of Making Something Simple to Understand

Isn't that exactly what we want to do when talking with customers or when presenting to a group?

Here's how:

1. Clearly describe what they need to hear only; not what you think they need to know about your topic. There's a big difference.
2. Then gives lots of examples. They accelerate understanding, relate to people's worlds and make the unfamiliar…familiar.
3. Finally, make sure you provide lots of visuals, even if it is a flipchart drawing.

Why is it sometimes, you just get things, you understand something? These three steps will let you have the same power.

Using Visual Aids

Tips to Using Slides

The definition of a visual aid is that it is something for the audience to look at that helps them get the message. Once you designed the content and you know what you want to do, then is the time to consider any additional visual aids that might help.

Challenge yourself not to use slides all the time. Visuals can be created in people's heads with a well crafted story, a metaphor, an interaction exercise, a physical prop, demonstrations and so on. Don't forget you…you are the most important visual aid for the audience to see and trust and believe, not a piece of machinery that displays stuff on a screen. If you do use slides, and I believe they still have their place, here are some tips for you:

- Bin the PowerPoint standard clip art.
- In fact bin all clip art. People have seen them all before.
- Use photos instead. Invest in a DVD collection of photo clip art.
- Use movies.
- Use sound and voice clips, but don't overdo the sound effects.
- Instead of facts and stats, try showing these as a simple chart or graph.

- Get rid of all the clutter that goes with slides – if it doesn't aid the message don't use it and that includes logos.

The last point about slides. Have your running notes separate and don't rely on the slides being your notes. That's a recipe for Death by PowerPoint.

So there we have perfect presentation planning. We began with the objectives, the foundation of your talk, we moved onto the audience and time, followed by venue and then content and finally visual aids. Follow the template next time you have a presentation to do. Stick to it and you'll be amazed by the results you can achieve.

PowerPoint Presentations

The traditional process to construct a presentation.

Recognise this process when you're putting together a presentation:

1. Find an old PowerPoint presentation that worked well.
2. Discard the slides that don't fit.
3. Add some new slides.
4. Re-order them into a structure.
5. Decide what narrative to say for each slide.

It's a recipe for a PowerPoint-dominated presentation with you providing additional information, or worse still, narrating the content of the slides. Because they may have a lot of information on them, people ask for copies, and we duly oblige, printing four slides per page. And heavens to Betsy, we might even give them out before the presentation.

During the presentation, you may follow this pattern:

1. Click onto the first slide…talk.
2. Click onto the second slide…talk.
3. Click onto the third slide…talk.

The slides are not visual aids. They are the structure, the points, the content, the lists, the bullets, graphs, maybe some photographs and clip art to make them more visual, but they are essentially…your notes…in the forms of bulleted lists.

You might have the bullet lists animated by coming in from the left, one by one, so you go to:

1. Reveal line…talk.
2. Reveal line…talk.
3. Reveal line…talk.

And substantial research shows this doesn't work. People remember very little of the presentation. Your audience may shut down and hope they don't have to endure any more death by PowerPoint.

I'm sure you're not like that, but you see my point. As a presenter, you deliver your content imperiously, ensuring the audience remembers the content and takes action. You have to battle hard to combat the slides.

But it's still not a visual presentation…it's a presentation with some visual aids. Big difference, so let's look at a way of achieving this.

Here's the new process if you want to have visual presentations, and you may want to make a number of changes to how you plan and prepare your talks.

The new process to construct a visual presentation:

Set your objectives of the presentation.

1. Select the right method.
2. Organise a presentation structure.
3. Decide the content.
4. Visualise it.
5. Design and animate the slides.
6. Practise.

Let's dive into each one, focusing on your PowerPoint since that's the purpose of this article.

Set your objectives

Not a lot for me to say on this except do it. Consider what your audience really needs to achieve, not what you want to talk about. What do they want to understand? What do they want to be able to do, to commit to, or agree to? Know your audience well and determine the timing. That's the three prongs – objectives, audience, and timing.

Select the Right Method

A stand-up presentation might not be correct. A webinar might be better, a white paper, a telephone conference, a one-to-one.

Organise the Structure

I mindmap my presentation structure as this starts my visualisation. You need to become heavily visual shortly, so it's good to start with structure. Standard structure…introduction and gain interest, make your first point, second point, third point, questions, and summary. If it's a sales presentation – state the problem or pain being experienced, your solution with proof, and a call to action.

Decide Content

Only include content that they really do need to achieve their objectives, not “filler” or “this might be useful” or this “might add value”. Just what they need to achieve the objectives. Then remove 20% of the content.

Now the fun part…

Visualise it

Presenting text on a screen doesn’t work. Words alone are not going to cut it as we’ve already seen; besides, you want to avoid text-only slides with the occasional piece of clipart. Every message can be visualised.

Think about the topic and contemplate how you can turn it into a graphic of some sort. Don’t worry about PowerPoint’s capability; that’ll come later. Just think how you could turn this content into a visual depiction.

Think of a graphic that can be built on screen, animated to grow in front of the audience’s eyes. Each click of the mouse does something on the screen, either building, moving, fading, highlighting, zooming in or out, and transitioning from one part of the picture to another.

Maybe it’s a photograph to provide a visual depiction. Possibly a pie chart, a Venn diagram, a pyramid, a map, bar charts.

Describe your message and make it visual. Think of animation or movement, not to distract or to look fancy, but purely to draw the audience’s attention to a particular point, to control their focus. The purpose is to control what they see and when, and you talk through each movement or transition.

There’s always a picture behind the content and message; you just need to look for it.

Design and Animate Your Slides

Remember; resist worrying about what you think PowerPoint is capable of. You can get someone else to do that. Learn or speak to me, I'll show you. The latest version of PowerPoint can do things that a couple of years ago would have taken armies of Photoshop experts and flash programmers to create.

Templates work well to give consistency of colours, brand, and such. But don't be tethered to the standard bullet lists, we want to get away from those.

Like most busy and frazzled business people you probably only use about 10% of PowerPoint's capability. That's not an insult; it's a fact for many. With some training you can learn:

- Shortcuts, tools, and personalised toolbar setup.
- Using media – shapes, charts, photos, SmartArt. Inserting and customising.
- Advanced photo formatting.
- Animation combinations and precise motion paths – the various static and motion builds available for the slideshow.
- Chart and graph animations.
- Embedding video and audio.

Practise

With all the animation and movement at every click, you'll want to practise a whole lot more because there are no sentences and lists for you to read from. But you wanted a more professional and engaging presentation, didn't you?

Practise so you know what's going on behind you and then practise some more.

You now have a visual presentation, not a presentation with the occasional visual aid.

The PowerPoint Dilemma

PowerPoint – you either love it or hate it. However, most people agree that badly produced slides are an anathema in business presentations, causing more anguish than Spanish Flu to audiences.

The problem is the template system which PowerPoint so handily provides. People use it because it makes creating text laden slides easy. We get text laden slides and they're not visual aids at all, they're merely the notes for speakers who can't be bothered to practise and know their presentation.

Get into graphs and charts and we're on a detail fest.

No, PowerPoint should be the vehicle for your visual aids. You could use any of the presentation software packages to achieve this, but you must start to think visually.

Humans want to listen to you and have some visual stimulus to help them understand the topic and engage more. It's as simple as that. Start by imagining you're standing to your screen's left hand side, the right side for an audience member. You begin presenting and your visuals pop up seamlessly and in time with your words. The images and visuals move, every 15 seconds something is animated or crosses in time with your words. The audience glances at the imagery and you in sequence and your message sticks.

Here's how:

Think through your presentation and visualise it. Imagine how it would appear if it were an animation. I like to picture board mine, drawing hand images that show the message and I indicate the movement that the images will make.

Next is to master PowerPoint's animation app. This allows you to move objects around in a myriad of ways. Only objects can be moved around or photos that you insert onto the page. Objects are shapes that can be accessed from the toolbar. In the screen dump below you can see some simple objects:

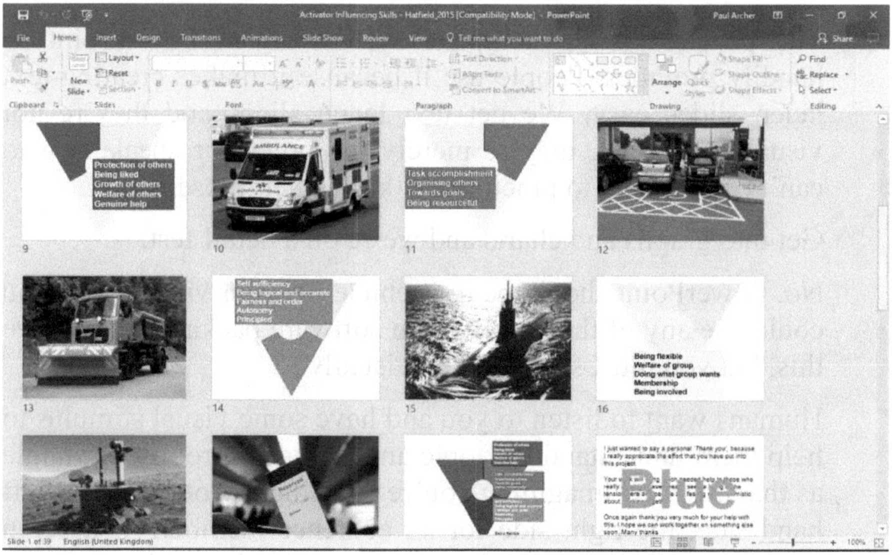

Here's a look at the various shapes you can use:

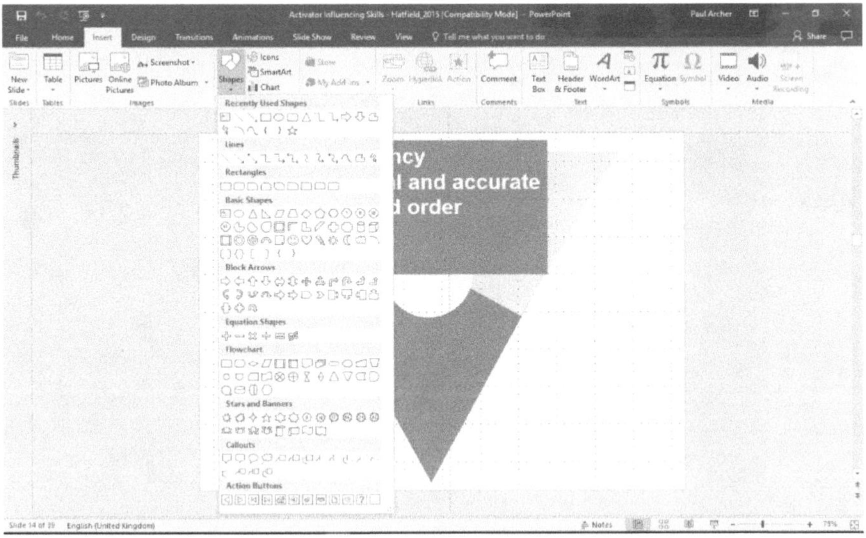

Now you can start to think about animating the shapes. You do this using animation and broadly there are three steps in an animation. The three motion paths are into the page, on the page and when it leaves the page. You can make them do virtually anything, so just experiment. You can also animate any photograph or imported graphic you care to use. If you put your text inside a box or shape, then you can even animate that.

Now you may want to short cut the design process using SmartArt.

Some smart person at Microsoft has played around with the various objects from earlier and has combined them for you, to save time. And they've put together hundreds for you to choose. These things are brilliant and you can even automate the animation of the whole collection with one click of the button. Here's how they look. Experiment and have fun:

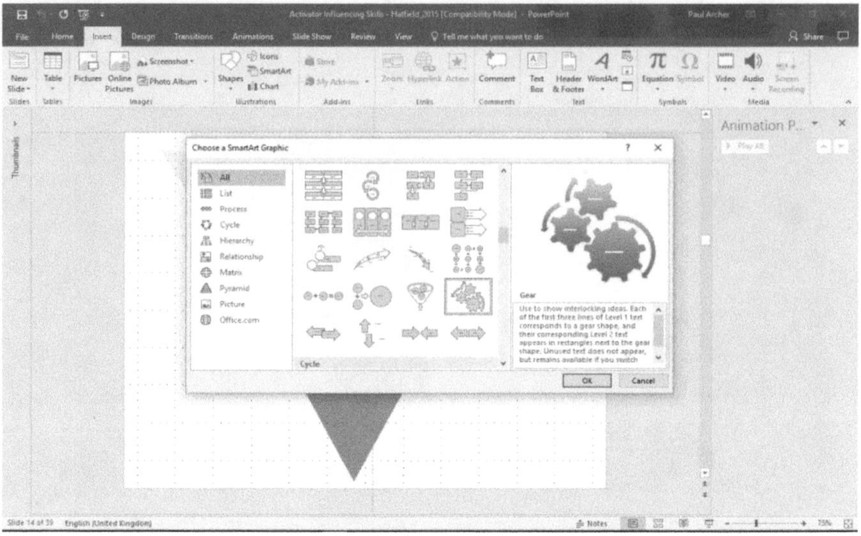

Charts can be visually presented using the Chart icon. Just add your data and the chart is produced. You can animate these easily so different bars appear at different times to aid your description of the data.

Now you might want to think about inserting video clips. That's easy to do and you can persuade the video to automatically play in full screen on a mouse click. Just beware of copyright issues if you like to trawl YouTube.

PowerPoint, you either love it or hate it. Using the concept of visualisation will allow your audience to love yours and remember your message.

Twenty-One Final PowerPoint Tips

1. Talk to your audience, not the screen. Trust the image behind you. Look at the laptop screen in front of you if you have to.

2. Stand centre stage and put the screen off to the side.
3. Place the screen at a slight angle on the left side of the room or stage (and to your right). Adult learning research shows that people use the left-brain to process data, so put PowerPoint words, statistics, and graphs on the audience's left.

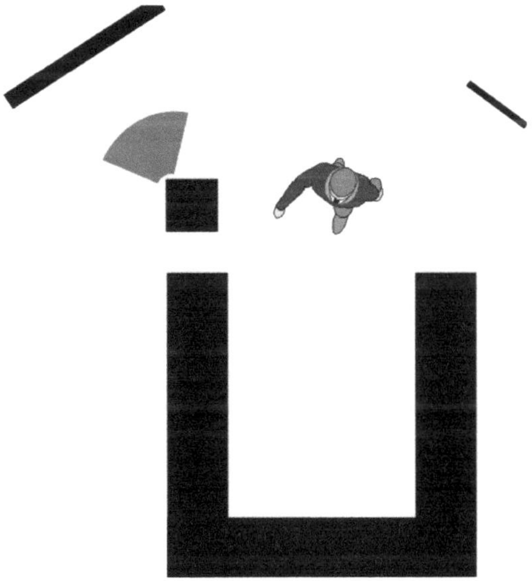

4. Learn to command your equipment. When in 'slideshow', the B key toggles to a blank screen (or W for white) when visuals aren't required. For more navigation tips, click F1.
5. A number followed by ENTER takes you to that slide. Keep a clearly numbered paper copy (nine slides per page) of your presentation so you can be flexible. Use the print command in PowerPoint.

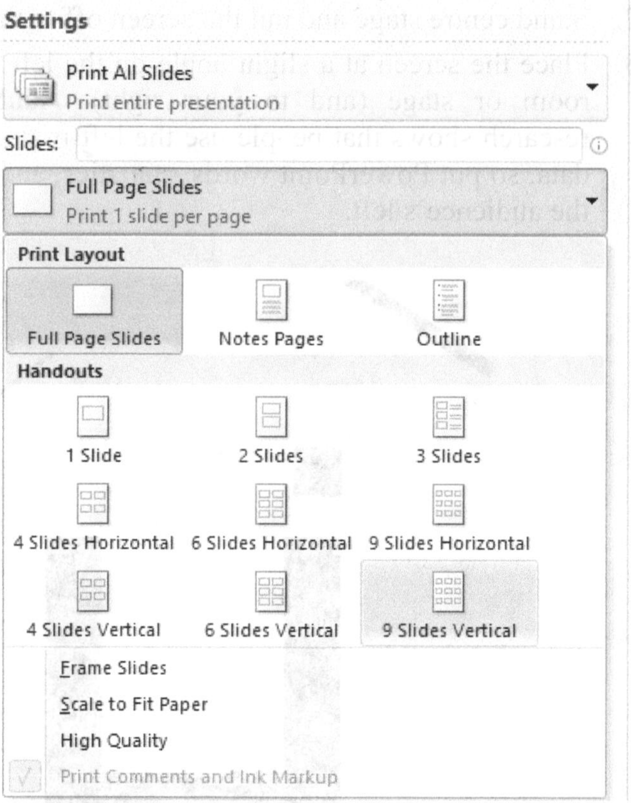

6. Set up your PC so that the left mouse button takes you forward, the right button takes you back a slide.
7. Finish with a blank slide at the end.
8. Put only enough data on each slide to jog your memory. The content should be in your head, not on the slides. Keep it simple.
9. If you have a busy set of slides which you have to use, then create an executive summary set to use whilst presenting and keep the busy set as handouts.
10. Avoid stock templates that just look cheap.

11. Use a wireless remote to give you freedom of movement. Buy the smallest you can and learn to keep it in the centre of your palm so as not to fiddle with it. Alternatively put it in your back pocket when not using.
12. Definitely no fancy movement or sound effects. These are so embarrassing.
13. If you just have to use a busy slide set, then use TTT (touch, turn, talk) to isolate the section you want and maybe adapt a new slide which just shows that section blown up. This way your audience knows that the slide with the detail is still there as a handout.
14. Have each bullet point slide onto the screen one at a time so people can read it quickly and give their attention back to you as you explain it.
15. Summarise charts and graphs that are difficult to understand.
16. Don't clutter the slide - use two slides instead.
17. Use white or yellow letters on a dark background for good contrast. Dark blue is attractive and colourful at the same time.
18. The letters should be no smaller than a 26-point, sans serif font.
19. Use the 1:6:6 rule. One subject, no more than six lines with no more than six words per line.
20. Don't use canned clipart that everyone has seen. Use different clipart collections. Better still, use photos and movies for added interest. But don't clutter the slides with your technical brilliance.
21. If a slide doesn't add value to your message, don't use it.

Alternatives to PowerPoint

In 2014, the England Football Team finished in their worst position of any World Cup since records began and has become synonymous with failure at national events.

Oh dear.

The same fate awaits PowerPoint. However well we use it, PowerPoint is now synonymous with boring, bullet driven snooze time.

Now, of course it's not always like that, some are excellent, but most business PowerPoint presentations fit that England Football team bill.

Here are some suggestions to be different, to cast away the anchor that is PowerPoint:

1. Prezi. Try this new piece of software. Essentially it's no different to PowerPoint when you get down to it but it does encourage movement, visual, imagination and that's a good thing. My advice is to purchase the desktop version rather than the cloud version as this gives you more flexibility whilst in boardrooms.
2. Whiteboards. I love whiteboards. I think they're terrific at building a picture, a diagram, a graphic representation of your presentation. They also make you out to be more of an expert in people's minds because you're creating an image in front of your audience. There's a new genre called "Whiteboard Sales" where salespeople use the whiteboard rather than PowerPoint to back up their presentation.
3. Use visually powerful language instead of any visual aids. Plenty of stories, metaphors and language which

encourage your audience to visualise the points you're making. Don't be afraid to use stories even in the stuffiest boardrooms, you'll be surprised that even C Suite Executives appreciate them.

PowerPoint or the alternative Keynote have lost their way, not because you can't make them visually involving and engaging, because you can. The word PowerPoint has been anchored and can't be changed. Instead, introduce your Prezi or whiteboard and you'll have your audience sit up and watch.

Prezi – An Alternative to PowerPoint

A study from Internet security firm AVG has found that more children between the ages of two and five can play with a smartphone app than can tie their shoes. The percentages are 19% to 9%.

Fascinating, and our personal anecdotal evidence can prove this. These are children of the digital age, and our very own Generation Ys are well into the workplace now.

So, have you considered how visual your PowerPoints are on your training courses? Do you have photos, images, movement, and visual metaphor sprinkled throughout your PowerPoint? Or do you have text and bullets sprinkled amongst your slides?

Rhetorical question, that last one, but if you have, you might consider using Prezi instead for your visuals.

Prezi is a cloud based presentation software that can completely visualise your topic. I've been using Prezi now for over three years, and it's really made a difference to some of my presentations and training events.

Try it, www.prezi.com.

Have you Used Uber?

It's the app for your phone that's taking over the world's city transportation. And if you're a cab driver, you'll be up in arms about them taking over your business.

But I'm not going to debate that issue, just how good their app is.

When you call a cab, you can see on a map, in real time, the arrival of your car. You see it graphically moving along the road until it reaches your destination. No need for words or descriptions, just pure visual.

How good is your visual?

How much visual do you provide in your coaching sessions? Do you create diagrams; use an iPad to show graphics and pictures, photos?

What about in selling? Perhaps you carry around a packet of whiteboard pens and you draw illustrations on the boardroom whiteboard rather than boring people with a whirring PowerPoint.

And your PowerPoints? Yes they are mostly pictures, images and photos aren't they?

In your webinars and Skype sessions, do you take every opportunity to show a graphic rather than talking, maybe share your screen if that serves to visualise? You can even have your video on the screen, that's visual.

In telephone seminars, you could ask the audience to join you on a padlet. Padlet.com is a useful app that allows your audience to interact on the screen whilst the seminar is running.

Everybody expects visual nowadays, Uber have shown this to the transportation industry which, sadly, is being left behind in their wake.

Are you?

It’s PowerPoint Pecha Kucha Style

You’ve probably heard it called Pecha Kucha; I prefer to call it 10/20/30 PowerPoint.

What’s the problem with PowerPoint? Nothing, the software is fabulous, bought from a little known company called Forethought Inc by Microsoft for $14m in 1989. Recently it's claimed to be loaded on 1 billion computers, dominating with a 95% market share of the presentation field.

The major downside is the ubiquitous use of bullets and if you didn’t know, bullets have a habit of killing people and many have been slain by bullet driven presentations.

Now 10/20/30 PowerPoint solves this problem and Pecha Kucha has taken it to a new level. Let me explain.

10 slides only, delivered for 20 minutes and no fonts less than 30 points. This ensures that large type is used and not too many lines of text dominate. Pecha Kucha takes it to the next level by automating the slides to change every 20 seconds but at least it allows 20 slides over a 400 second presentation.

This creates a number of benefits for the audience. It forces the presenter to cut to the chase and eliminates waffle. It ensures the presenter practises their presentation, which is always highly recommended. Most slides end up being very visual or with very large text, so it's nigh on impossible to run a bullet laden slide over 20 seconds. It makes sure no presenter ever overruns – a common annoyance for audiences and the next speaker, I can tell you from experience.

Presenters stick to the story and the story is easily digested by the audience.

And not a bullet in sight.

Such a blessed relief.

In Iran I Stood to the Right of the Screen

In the USA I stood to the left of the screen, in Bangladesh I had no choice.

People often ask me, which side of the screen should the presenter stand? As if it makes a difference? And it does.

Often this is determined by the room size and position of any fixed screen or projector, but if you have a choice you should adopt the reading pattern of your audience.

You see in many countries we read from left to right, we have done since we entered primary school and this subconscious habit governs how we gaze at the presenter and the information she is sharing on a screen at the front of the room.

In the UK we read from left to right, so stand to the left of the screen, facing the audience and point to your visual aid which will be to the right of the audience. If you want proof, watch the BBC Weather and the presenter is always standing to the left of the map of the country as he points out cold fronts and precipitations using his left arm and the audience gazes from left to right just as if they were reading a magazine.

When presenting your visuals, follow the weatherman's techniques. He'll be keeping eye contact with the camera, and likewise, you should keep eye contact with the audience as you point out aspects of your visual.

I use the TTT method – touch, turn and then talk. So touch the area of the visual you want to highlight, then turn your head to the audience and finally talk. Touch, turn and talk.

Better still, let the animation built into your visual do the pointing out for you.

If you ever have the opportunity to present to an audience that reads right to left such as Iran or Saudi Arabia, then you simply swap positions. It's the sign of a professional.

But sometimes the room design leaves you with no choice, and that happened to me at a presentation in Bangladesh, but this is such a subtle technique, nobody really noticed at all.

Stories in Business Presentations

There are numerous methods of delivering content in a presentation, although many presenters lean on just one or two methods. Seasoned presenters deliver content in a wide variety of means and the very best of them use stories to illustrate their points.

The stories we use are not made up on the fly, they are crafted, practised and delivered in the same way each time. They serve one point, are sequenced and follow a distinct structure. The whole rationale of a story is that the point you're making must flow logically at the end.

Stories must come from your past, either personal or business. A good business story will demonstrate your credibility yet a solid personal story will show the audience that you are real and can relate business points to personal situations – it's more human. The important aspect is that it must be your story, be true and illustrate you in action.

Do you admire paintings? I'm sure you do. The kind of artist I admire is John Constable or Claude Monet. These artists paint with a fine brush and have an incredible attention to detail, almost to the point when you might confuse the painting with a photograph. I admire their talent. In the same way, when you tell a story in a presentation you must use a fine brush, not a roller. The magic is in the detail.

Story Structure

Allow me to tell you a story which I've told many times and which pretty much flows in the same way every time. Then I'll unpack it and illustrate the structure you should use when crafting your stories.

Before we go there, a word or two about duration. You can be brave here and spend a few minutes with a story. If your structure is sound, engaging and a firm point evolves that brings value to the audience, then spend the time. Stories that lack these qualities soon annoy the audience; you see it in their faces so you rush the story.

Unsurprisingly the story's point must be linked to the session's objectives, usually to prove a point or illustrate a concept.

Naturally it depends how long you have available to talk and this will also determine how many stories you embed. A typical 45 minutes for me might include 4 or 5 stories, each lasting around 2 to 3 minutes.

Mondays are always hectic, especially the morning routine when you just seem to be late for everything. It was freezing cold that November morning and still pitch black outside when I learnt Bethan was having an inset day and wasn't going to school. So I became a baby sitter for my ten year old daughter, although I had stacks to do that day.

Bethan had the run of the house for the whole day. TV whenever she wanted it, laptops to play on, the fridge was all hers and her two arch enemies – her two older brothers – were safely locked away in school. So I kept my office door open and listened out for her whenever I could. But she was fine.

My day was going very much to plan and the next item on my to-do list was a run. I try to go for a run every day or so for 45 minutes, and since I was going to be working away for a few days, this was to be the last run before then, so I really wanted to do it today.

How could I leave my daughter on her own at home? But my urge to run got the better of me, besides, I run along the fields around my house so I was always available and I thought I'd take my phone just in case. She'd be fine.

I promised Bethan I wouldn't be long and headed off for my run down the lane alongside the house, and turned right across a field right opposite my house. At the bottom of the field I normally stop to do a stretch or two on my aging muscles. From here I can clearly see the house. I looked up and saw, from a distance, Bethan at the front door, waving at me.

Or was she waving for me to return? Was she in trouble? Was she frightened and wanting me to come back home? Thoughts rushed through my mind. What have I done, poor Bethan she's in danger, what a terrible daddy I am. I must rush back and rescue her. So I sprinted as fast as my legs would take me.

Gasping for breath at the door I shouted to see if she was OK. "Of course I'm OK Daddy, I was just waving at you."

"But I thought you were in trouble so I came rushing back to see."

"Daddy, it's your fault," said Bethan, "It's your thought."

Later that day on my second attempt at a run, those words resonated with me. Bethan was spot on. It was totally my fault that I thought that way, I'm in control of my thoughts, no one else and I chose to think that she was in danger when she was harmlessly waving at me.

You see, we are in control of our thoughts, whether we realise it or not, so next time you're having negative destructive thoughts that serve no purpose, stop yourself, chuck them out, and control your thinking.

Now before you go and phone Child Line to report me, at least I did worry about her before my run, and I did sprint back to rescue her!

Let me unpack the story around the structure:

- Set the scene
- Introduce the characters
- Begin the journey
- Encounter the obstacle
- Resolve the story
- Make the point
- Ask the question

Set the scene. This is the time to help the audience create the situation in their heads because they will want to. Here there's an attention to detail – time, place, weather, conditions. In my story you knew it was spring, a bright day, mid-week, my home office. You could see the hill where I was living surrounded by green countryside.

Introduce the characters. Again the detail matters. You know me but I added that I operated by self-talk, giving myself deadlines and goals and used a to-do list. This drove me to action, you now know that. You know Bethan, a 10-year-old, self-sufficient, enjoying her unexpected day off, spending time with her Dad.

Begin the journey. This is not always a physical journey, it can be a quest, a journey towards a resolution. For me it was to achieve my timed run without Bethan falling into danger and overcoming the nagging fear in my head of making a terrible decision.

Encounter the obstacle. This is the solution to the story. You can either overcome it or fail. Failure is good, more learnings evolve from failure. I failed in the story. My inner dialogue got the better of me and I began to believe what I was making up in my head.

Resolve the story. Here you need to tie up any loose ends. In my story, Bethan announces “Daddy I’m fine, I was just waving to say I love you”.

Make the point. One clear point that progresses into the learning or moral is – the phrase that pays. Bethan announcing “It's your fault Daddy, it's your thought” became both the learning and the key phrase that pays.

Ask the question. Ask the audience about their reference to the point, how do they deal with the issue and repeat the phrase that pays once more.

There, I’ve unpacked it for you. Shall I tell you another and see where the structure develops.

It was 11 o’clock in the evening on a hot sticky evening in July and I was driving from my home in Gloucestershire to Bradford. My aim was to get to my hotel so I could get my standard 8 hours sleep. Now that was my first failing that day. Oh, I forgot to mention, I was driving my wife’s car, a very fast Peugeot SXi hot hatchback and I was dressed in shorts, tee shirt and a baseball cap. My son said earlier that Daddy looked a little bit cool.

I’d failed on my 8 hour sleep target since I’d just left a two hour jam around Manchester. I was at the highest motorway point in the UK; between Bradford and Manchester on the M62. I was at the highest point and it appeared to be downhill from there.

I was tired, frustrated and keen to get to my hotel. I looked ahead and oh no, another set of road works. The next thing I knew in my rear-view mirror was that familiar sight of flashing blue lights.

PC Bird whistle was a young policeman. Immaculate in his uniform, tall and with a subtle Sheffield accent. He looked as though he was born to be a policeman, and a traffic cop at that. He invited me into his car as you and I would invite someone into their home. He was perfectly polite as though my mum had taught him his Ps and Qs.

As I sat in the back of that Volvo, watching the video of me speeding into the roadworks, I'd hoped not to get a ticket by being polite and subservient. It didn't work. He began to fill in the ticket and I'd resigned myself to 3 points and a £65 fine.

- Address? High House, Prior's Norton, Gloucestershire
- Occupation? Company Director
- What do you do? I run my own training and consultancy company

He then looked at me in a surprised manner. It suddenly dawned on me: my car, my uniform, my short hair. His impression of me was coloured before I even got out of the car.

I asked him.

"Before I go, tell me, out of curiosity, if I'd been driving my Mondeo and I was wearing my suit, would you have booked me?"

He then looked at me with a twinkle in his eye. "I'll escort you back to your car Sir."

His first impression had let me down. How many times do you give people the wrong first impression and how often do we arrive at a visual first impression wrongly.

Think first impressions.

Story Delivery

Stories delivered from your stage need to be acted out using all the space and thespian skills you can muster. This also emphasises the need to practise not just the words and structure, but how you physically deliver it.

Act out your characters. Move slightly when being one person, then adjust your position when narrating the other character.

Act out the scene. When I tell the story with my daughter, I put my right leg on the back of a chair and do leg stretches in front of the audience. As I'm sprinting up the lane, I imitate this in slow motion so they can see me running. As I arrive at the front door I bend over panting as though I've just finished a 200 metre sprint and breathe heavily as I ask Bethan how she is.

I also come in and out of the story. When I need to narrate, I will, for example when I was setting the scene in driving to Bradford or the weather where I used to live. But I stepped back into the story when I was visualising the rush of a 45-tonne articulated lorry passing by.

Use your voice to good effect. Fast or slow. Speed up your delivery when you want some action, some excitement. My voice sped up when I was released from the road works or when I was rushing home to rescue my daughter. Slow down to emphasise important moments. When Bethan announced she was fine and it was my fault, I slowed right down.

Choreograph your story. Remember the audience are listening of course, their internal imagination is running riot but they are also watching you and seeing your acting only adds that extra sparkle to the story.

It's worth practising the art of storytelling. You'll stand out amongst your colleagues, your audience will enjoy your stories and they'll remember the message.

The rest of this chapter is devoted to a selection of my favourite stories to illustrate a point, for you to enjoy and to demonstrate further the sequence and methods I've shown you.

Rapport is Common Ground

A couple of years ago I lived on a typical family estate with 3 and 4 bedroom homes, each with three children, two dogs and one barbeque. Every November I received a box of poppies from the Royal British Legion and I would knock on doors to see how many poppies I could sell.

Each year I raised a consistent £35 or so.

People weren't reticent about buying poppies, after all it's an amazing cause. The problem was that many people had already bought their poppy or had signed up to a standing order or always bought one from a favourite seller. So I had to be happy with my £35.

But one year I decided a different tactic and thought about building a rapport with my customers. At the time, my son Lewis was aged 5 and actually rather cute. He's now turned into a teenager so is now rather frightening.

I decided to take him with me so decked him out with the posters of rank, a box of poppies around his waist and a cute bobble hat.

And what happened next was amazing.

The first door I knocked on, the man of the house came to the door, looked at me and quickly realised that I was selling poppies, then he glanced at Lewis and I could read the man's mind.

"Ah", he thought, "this man is selling poppies…I already have my poppy…how can I turn him down. But hold on…he has a son about the age of my son…he's a dad like me…we have something in common…I like this man…he's just like me…where's my wallet?"

That night I made £78.50. Same road, same houses, same people, but I doubled my takings.

The simple fact was that I was showing my customers that I was the same as them; I was building a common ground. You see people like to deal with people who are the same as them and have done so for thousands of years.

Learn to Let Go

We have an acre paddock next to our house and this year I inherited a second hand sit on mower from my father who no longer needed it. For the first few months I enjoyed driving the mower around the field having a great time. A Briggs and Stratton engine with 12 horse power, effortlessly cutting swathes of grass on every turn with a top speed of 8 MPH and a metre-long cutting blade that rotates at tremendous speeds.

She's a beast.

But like most men with their new toys, the novelty soon wore off and it became a chore.

Eureka, I spotted my eldest son kicking stones looking to earn some money for his holiday. Now Lewis is 14 and quite capable, but I was a little fearful for my first born on top of this monster and took to giving him plenty of lessons and guidance on how to navigate the field, work the gears and understand the safety aspects, while at the same time showing him how to cut neat lines like my wife likes. I was determined to put all my training skills into practice to give him the very best education.

But then I realised that he just needed to have a go without me hovering over him. Just let him have a go and make mistakes and trust that he'll sort it out himself.

It was difficult to wrench myself away and just let him drive the machine. Sometimes when coaching, you just have to let go.

So next time you're training or coaching someone, let go a little earlier than you would normally do and revel in the difference it makes to your coachee. Yes, be on hand to help, but let go of the helicopter approach to sales management.

Learn to let go.

And Lewis, how did he get on? A few wobbly moments, some decidedly skewed lines, some stalled engines, plenty of Mohican strips…but on the whole a great first month and with a little gentle feedback from me, he has begun to master the art of lawn cutting.

Next step - the hedge.

Life's a Rollercoaster

I'd never travelled on a rollercoaster. Honest, I know it sounds remarkable, but I'd never had the courage to climb into the small cab and ride the heart wrenching and stomach churning experience.

Until one afternoon over Christmas when my youngest son dared me to get on the ride at Poulton's Park. Now if you ever want to motivate me to do something, you only need to dare me. I think it's hard wired into most men.

I watched Euan first and thought I'd use the 1st, 2nd, 3rd position that we use all the time when selling. Now this clever little tip helps you see, feel and fully understand what it's like for someone else and in sales, is a useful way of exploring the customer's point of view.

1st position is where you look at things through your own eyes and as I stared at Euan on the rollercoaster, all I could think of was fear, trepidation, how foolish, help!

2nd position is where you step out of your shoes and move into the customer's shoes and look at thinks through this person's eyes, in other words see and feel their point of view. So I tried this and moved into Euan's shoes. Initially I could still feel my fear and trepidation, but I kept at it and began to see how Euan saw the ride. He was smiling and cheering so loud I could hear him from where I was standing. As he approached the top of the loop just before he was to plunge downwards at breath-taking speed, his look was of apprehension but total excitement. He was enjoying the thrill of the ride and I started to feel what this was like for him.

3rd position is where you stand back, disassociate yourself from both viewpoints and look objectively at the situation. With customers, we get to see their views and yours in tandem. On the rollercoaster I could see Euan's viewpoint, mine and the other passengers on the coaster. I realised that everyone seemed to be having fun and that this miserable father was seeing the rollercoaster in a very blinkered way.

And did I enjoy it? Yes I did, and I had to go on it again and again. In fact since it wasn't too busy, I went on the same ride 3 times and Euan now thinks his Dad is real cool.

So next time you really want to appreciate your customer's point of view, go from 1st position, to 2nd and then finally to 3rd position.

The Mackerel Trawler

All summer Lewis and Euan kept badgering me to take them mackerel fishing. There seemed something adventurous and mysterious about heading out to the open sea in a real fishing trawler to catch mackerel and bring them home for breakfast.

I caved in to their demands during our weeks visit to Salcombe, Devon this summer. I was really quite looking forward to it myself, if truth be told, but I kept them dangling on the hook, so to speak, to boost their enthusiasm.

It was a damp Monday morning in mid-August when we set off on the good ship Calypso from Salcombe harbour.

It was early and very overcast, with a smattering of drizzle, but not too windy. Besides we were wrapped up, dry and had just parted company with £35 in cash to the eager boat owner.

Out we sailed, fairly calm it was, and a few other boats were sailing along the estuary. It was the height of the tourist season and every Brit seemed to be "stay-cationing" in the UK this year, so it was quite busy. The views were stunning. Salcombe has a natural harbour in its estuary, the hills on either side rise sharply to provide an excellent shelter for the myriad of boats, yachts and ships that ply their trade along the coast.

The boys were having a great time. Excited, eager to catch breakfast and holding on to the sides bolstered by their life jackets. I was enjoying the scenery and the skills of the captain. I always admire a man at the top of his game. Our grizzled and weathered captain had many years' experience, you could tell.

And a good job he had too, as it turned out.

Still within the confines of the estuary, Euan shouted to the captain "Can we fish here?"

"No, young sir, no mackerel here, we have to go further out."

As we left the sanctuary of the estuary the whole outlook changed, the winds picked up, the swells increased and the waves started rising alarmingly towards us. The trawler which looked so strong and worthy in the safety of the harbour suddenly looked bewildered and vulnerable in the open sea and we rode the swells in alarming fashion.

The boys held on for their lives and so did I, but the captain assured us this was very unusual and he'd steam around the swells. I'm glad he was there.

You see in business – sales, coaching or managing – we often languish in our safety zone, not wanting to take risks or move beyond our comfort blanket, our known world. But if we do, it opens up new horizons. The salesperson who takes on a whole new client who he never dreamed of approaching, the sales coach who adopts a new style of coaching, a manager who takes a risk or two.

These can all lead to new zones which can provide fresh rewards.

The good boat Calypso was safe in its estuary but as soon as it entered the outside sea, it began to struggle. Thankfully we had the captain who was able to sail us around the swells to calmer sea, where we were able to relax a little. And then we could cast our hooks over the side and reel in mackerel after mackerel to take home for our breakfast. I wish it were always so.

So next time you feel you're stuck in your estuary and shelter, but don't seem to be making any headway, reach out and leave your comfort zone. You never know what riches you'll find.

And as for our catch, well for me it was non-existent. The sea picked up again, I lost my sea legs, felt terribly ill and laid down in the cabin for the duration of the trip, much to my embarrassment. I didn't catch a sprat. If it wasn't for the boys, we'd have had nothing to eat for breakfast; they were very successful as we steamed through shoal after shoal of mackerel.

So much for my Mackerel Fishing Adventure, but at least I experienced something outside my comfort zone!

Glastonbury

In 2006, I failed to get to the Glastonbury Festival. Awfully disappointed I was, especially as the festival approached, and the TV and the newspapers were saying what a brilliant Glasto it was going to be and one of my favourite bands – Blur – were going to headline.

So I decided to record every piece of Glastonbury that the BBC could show and watch the recordings over and over again as a consolation. The BBC probably shows about 50 hours in total of the festival, so using Sky Plus was out of the question since it doesn't have the capacity.

I picked up a new Archos Personal Video Recorder to attach to the TV to ensure I didn't miss one showing of the festival.

I'd cracked it – I could now relax and look forward to watching hour after hour of Glasto, whenever and wherever I liked.

Until my wife picked up the gadget and asked, what on earth do we need this for as we've got Sky Plus?

Patiently awaiting an answer, I told her "Darling, we can use it to do other TV recordings that stay recorded forever and not be wiped off by our adorable children, we can record movies to watch later, we can use it to store photos when we're on holiday this year when the camera card gets filled up, we can take it to your Mum's this Christmas and show lots of photos of the children by rigging it up to their TV. I can even use it for work to show delegates videos of their presentation."

Phew that was close.

But the point is this: It was a pure logical justification. I bought on emotion and justified the expenditure on logic to my wife and myself.

Customers buy on emotion and justify with logic later on.

So how much emotion do you bring into your sales meetings?

In total I must have recorded about 75 hours of Glastonbury. Have I seen it all? No way…can you remind me why I bought the Archos 400? Oh yes, it was hard-drive storage, the ability to record TV programmes permanently, photos at Christmas…

A Tale of Two Carts

Gloucester to Mansfield, with a change at Derby, meant two Intercity trains both with refreshment carts that I could choose from and enjoy. But what a difference in the way they were handled.

Cart Number One: Moving up and down the walkway. Quiet. Calling "Coffee, tea, hot chocolate?" Repetitive and apologetic, worried should people say no. Didn't want to be there.

Cart Number Two: Enthusiastic and believing in their value. "Who's peckish then?" "You like the look of my beverages don't you madam?" Cheeky, looking for opportunities, watching us, looking for signals, alert. If someone said no thanks, "Not a problem, but if you change your mind just holler", "It's that time, don't you think, for a cuppa", "Sir, I saw you peeking at my trolley, anything grab your attention?" "Why not treat yourself Sir, to a piece of cake with that tea?"

The parallels are everywhere in sales, particularly retail sales. These are people who are asked to cross sell products to customers calling into their space: Building society cashiers, PC World assistants, B&Q helpers, conservatory salespeople, IFAs.

The tip is to emulate our friend on the refreshment cart – it wasn't a particularly rewarding job, lots of potential rejection and repetitively wandering up and down. But don't take it too seriously, detach yourself a little from the pressure, show enthusiasm and then just look for opportunities like the gentleman caught sneaking a peek at his trolley; throw out some bait and just ask.

It's not that difficult to cross sell, we just make it so in our heads.

Asking for a Date

As a fully-fledged signed up member of the Union of Dads' Taxis, I was bringing my teenage son home from town with his new girlfriend last Saturday. They'd just been to the cinema on their first date and we were getting close to her home. It was pelting down with rain and as we approached her estate, I could hear my son attempting to ask her for another date.

It was a classic close the sale situation. "Just ask her" I was pleading in my head. Just ask the girl, her body language is saying it, just ask. Easy for me to say, but how easy is it to close the sale?

Closing has to be the hardest ask for any salesperson, customer adviser or counter assistant. Call us what you like, the pure fact is that if we sell for a living, the key decider for a salesperson is being able to ask the customer to go ahead. It's the same, whether it is Gemma in the back of the car or Mr Brown who is deciding about the annual travel policy you're selling.

Sometimes customers like to be directed and led to the close. They have learnt to trust you and regard you as the professional, so use this trust to move things along. Let's go back to the car and the conversation on the back seat.

Lewis; "Gemma, we both had a great time tonight didn't we, so shall we go out again next week?"

Gemma; "Lovely idea, Lewis."

If only it happened like that. Instead on my way home, I had a very confused teenage boy on the back seat on his own, staring out of the rain spattered window, wondering why he just didn't ask.

Remember to close.

The Windscreen Washer Nightmare

Last month I was travelling to a sales training event in Wales that I was running, with pretty good internal feelings and self-talk. It was a beautiful summer's morning crossing the Severn Bridge, I was on time, looking forward to the training, confident and enjoying the drive. Sun roof open, fresh air streaming through, I felt good…until the news came on the radio.

Legionnaires' disease was the main topic on the news. The latest research revealed that the most dangerous place to catch Legionnaires' disease wasn't hospitals or infected sky scrapers…but the car. Apparently the disease lives very happily in the windscreen washer bottle, being warm, still and the perfect place for the culture to grow. So all car drivers watch out, you could be in for a shock.

So how did I feel being about 1 metre from my windscreen bottle and having just sprayed the washer to clear off bugs on the windscreen? And did I have the sun roof open to let in the water vapour? You bet I did.

You see, how we feel is all to do with our self-talk and right then my self-talk wasn't worth printing and this made me feel low.

So how can we control this? It's not easy, you have to be strict with yourself but the trick is to control what you dwell on. I'm not suggesting that you blot out all negative thought in your head, that would be naïve and would probably put you in danger. No, you can control these by focusing just on the ones which you have control over and ditch the ones you can't control or influence.

Worrying about Legionnaires' disease didn't do me any favours, I can't stop it unless I wash the bottle in the engine every night with disinfectant and refill it every day, and I'm going to do that, right?

No, forget about it if you can't control it and move on. Focus your attention on the now and positive thoughts that you're planning for the future. Your goals, your objectives, your plans, and be wary of thinking about negative things that may never ever happen.

Control your self-talk.

Duke Nukem Ego

I've been a sucker for computer games ever since I bought Doom in 1991 for my first computer. And for the next 5 years I played them nonstop – Doom 1, Doom 2, Duke Nukem, my absolute favourite, I played them all to the early hours, until my first child arrived, my mortgage doubled and life became rather more serious.

I haven't played a game since, until this year, when Duke Nukem Forever was announced. I bought it without hesitation to reminisce and bring back those good times and for the next few days I played it constantly, much to my wife's annoyance.

I started speaking like Duke and acting like him. You see, Duke Nukem is a total hero; he bristles with muscles, sports a six pack, kills baddies with ease, is utterly attractive to women and has a massive ego. But Duke's ego is different to ours; it's his health and well-being. When he gets shot up, blown up with grenades, falls down tower blocks, he loses ego so has to quickly replenish it otherwise he'll die.

Get the metaphor?

Doing things and achieving tasks give him extra ego. Here are some examples:

- Clear Pool Table – In Duke's apartment. +2 Ego

- Mirror – Admire yourself in Duke's bathroom mirror. +1 Ego
- Autograph – Sign the fan's autograph. +2 Ego
- Score With Basketball – In gym after conference call. +1 Ego
- Bench Press – Need 6 weights on bench total. +3 Ego
- Punch bag – Punch the bag. +1 Ego
- Dumbbell – Curl the small weights. +1 Ego
- Slot Machine – Play until you win.+1 Ego

All the time you can see a dial which shows how much ego he has.

Duke's health is his ego. Salespeople's health is their ego or, as I prefer to call it, their self-esteem. Salespeople must have self-esteem, or self-belief, confidence in themselves. It's not arrogance that's self-belief on steroids. Duke gets away with arrogance, modern salespeople don't.

Can you measure your own or your salespeople's self-esteem levels? Do you coach them in improving their self-esteem, do you coach attitudes and beliefs rather than just skills?

How do you preserve your own self esteem? Duke plays games to win things and succeeds as often as he can. Do you? What do you do to maintain and increase your self-esteem? By believing in yourself, being confident, handling negative self-dialogue, harvesting praise, coping with negatives, only then will you have rock solid self-esteem, just like Duke.

Did I finish the Duke Nukem computer game? No way, my wife took it away from me; she couldn't cope any longer with me acting like Duke Nukem. "Watch out world, its Duke here", "I'm the greatest", "Everyone loves the Duke".

The Kennel Club

"You haven't, have you Paul?" "Yes we have" I replied. "We've 8 puppies and we're planning on selling 7 of them over the next month".

"You'll never sell them Paul; we had puppies last year and are still stuck with them all. Mark my words" was the warning.

I developed a sinking feeling in the pit of my stomach. How are we going to persuade 7 people to buy our puppies? There's no demand, we're in the middle of a recession, how would we cope with 8 puppies at home?

The next day we registered the puppies with the Kennel Club as they were pedigrees and you have to go through a strict process to adhere to their rules. As part of the agreement, you had to ensure that the puppies went to good homes, with fine owners who were going to treat them well, walk them daily and care for all their needs. We had a Kennel Club responsibility and had to prove that we'd done our due diligence on all the new owners.

This changed everything overnight. From wanting keenly to sell the puppies, we now wanted to find good owners for them all. From there on my wife started to interview prospective owners to see if they passed her "test of good ownership" and people became very enthusiastic to pass her test and become an owner of a Spinone puppy.

From being quite keen to sell, we became detached from the sale, so the pressure had fallen away. This made the product more appealing to prospective owners and sure enough, in the first weekend, we sold 4 and the last 3 quickly followed the following week.

What about you in selling? Are you too attached to your product or service? Are you too intense about selling, do you get a little too keen sometimes? Can you unattach yourself a tad, take the pressure off and make your proposition more desirable?

Detaching yourself is the key to increasing the desirability of your product. Just ask Brodie's 8 puppies who all found gorgeous homes, thanks to the Kennel Club rules.

Remember to detach yourself from the sale.

Potholing

"You need a hobby" were the last words from my wife's mouth as I left on an overseas trip. You see I'd been working all weekend preparing for my talk which is wrong, foolish and not good for the soul. Fortunately, on the plane, I browsed one of those flight magazines and came across an article on potholing. Fascinating.

If you ask questions as a coach or consultative salesperson, you need to ask good questions, not dumb ones. Obvious that, really. Dumb questions get you nowhere, they're often leading or multiple questions or just plain dumb.

In potholing this is where you aim down a narrow dead end. You have no choice but to retrace your steps back to where you started.

In potholing, if you find the right route, you can be rewarded with a cavern of stalagmites and stalactites, wondrous scenery and numerous further vistas to explore. Faced with this cavern, you just have to keep exploring.

It's the same in coaching. Power questions give you enormous amounts of information and colour that allow you to continue exploring. A powerful question is expansive and opens up further routes to explore for the coach. A power question is one where you get that look from your coachee or client. They're saying to themselves, "That's a good question", they look up and ponder the answer. And because you're good at listening and nodding, they give you an enlightened answer which by the mere process of verbalising it, has given them colossal value.

When I returned home a few days later armed with gifts for the whole family I announced the best present of all. "I'm going to join a pot holing club – The Gloucester Speleological Society, I've googled them and they are welcoming new members."

And the response? Well I daren't tell you, it's not publishable. Oh well, back to the drawing board for my hobby.

Pigeon Poo

Two years ago I made the mistake of parking in a hotel car park under a huge tree. When I returned to the car two days later it was covered in pigeon poo which had been burnt on by the mid-day sun. What a mess and I swore never to repeat the mistake.

During the next year of using the same car park, sure enough, I never repeated the same mistake.

But after a gap of almost a year, I returned to that same car park. I arrived late; I was tired and parked my car in the same space. And, yes I returned later to find my car completely covered in pigeon poo. I'd been grockled. Again.

What an error I thought, but then again was it? And this made me ponder about our worlds as salespeople and coaches:

There's no problem in repeating messages, after all people forget.

And my car? It was caked on this time, it took me three automatic car washes, two manual car washes and some elbow grease to get it clean.

The Gloucester Rugby Ball

When my son Euan was younger, he played for a junior rugby team and I helped to coach them alongside other keen and enthusiastic dads.

We were a reasonable team, not brilliant; I think the quality of the coaches was also in question. But we sought ways to improve. Serendipity provided the answer. Let me explain.

At the club's annual dinner, we were donated a rugby ball from Gloucester Rugby's 2005 winning team. An actual match ball used by top players. You know; it was felt, passed and caught by real players. The ball went into the auction as the top prize.

Let me fast-forward the story. We won the ball in the auction.

I thought that's it, at last we can play like winners, so I introduced the ball at our next training session and used it for the match against Kidderminster.

Did the ball make a difference? Not a bit. We lost handsomely.

A ball is not going to make any difference. Responsibility for performance lies with the players and the coaching team; we hadn't improved and a new ball wasn't going to make any transformation.

In the same way, responsibility in coaching lies with the coachee not the coach.

Camping in France

It was a scorching afternoon in the Vendee, France at Les Dunes Camping Site. We'd just arrived after a long drive and Sharon, our Rep, was showing us to our caravan which was to be home for a few weeks. Now this is always a scary moment as you are in their hands for the choice of location.

Would we be next to the family from hell?

Would we be next to the bar or worse still, the Karaoke?

No, we were being led back towards the entrance to the park, with the main road and amusements. Before I even thought of the noise issue, the Rep turned around and said confidently.

"The people before you were a little worried about being close to the entrance but when they left yesterday they told me what a great location they had. They mentioned how close the van was to all the amenities and how quiet it was at night."

I hadn't even thought about the noise problem until she mentioned it but because she'd given me a customer testimonial and some benefits of the location, it didn't even cross my mind that it would be a quandary.

Clever girl.

I wonder if she was a trained salesperson. But the point was she did just the right thing. Let me explain further.

No product or service is perfect. There are always downsides or disadvantages or the competition has the edge in one or two areas. No one has a "killer application" for long these days as competition is so swift and reactive.

There's always going to be something the customer might not fully appreciate and just might lead to an objection later on, usually when we ask for the order or close the sale.

Now I'm not saying that you should tell the customer all the main problems of your product early on in the process. What I'm saying is, if there is a particular feature that the competition beat you on, and previous customers have mentioned it before, then pre-empt it.

Just like Sharon did with the caravan location.

It might not be a problem with your product or service. It could just be a hurdle your customer has to cross before they can enjoy the product. Something that potentially might cause them to stall when it comes to purchasing.

The Lodger

It was the summer of 1992, Dee Lite was topping the charts, the world-wide web hadn't even been invented and phones were firmly strapped to the wall of your house.

I found myself caught in the worst property recession known. Prices had plummeted by over 30% and the house I owned suffered this fate. Negative equity they called it. Your mortgage was more than the value of your home and you were stuck.

I needed to move, so I rented a place near my work and let out my room to lodgers. The good news was that our Prime Minister at the time, the flamboyant John Major, ensured the income from your rent was tax free, but the bad news was you needed to collect rent from lodgers.

Collecting rent from a lodger is strewn with problems especially when they paid in cash. The problem I had was getting them to pay each month. I had all the excuses known thrown at me. “Haven’t got the cash at the moment, give me a couple of days” or “Cheque's in the post” or “My overtime’s not come in this month, can I pay you double next month?”

Until I hit on an idea. You see, I’m one of life’s nice guys, I don’t particularly like conflict, I steer clear of it and every month I would dread collecting the rent. So with a new lodger, I explained that I was acting on behalf of the new landlord, who lived in Edinburgh, Scotland. I was his buddy.

Sure enough the same excuse came from my new lodger but this time I used the line:

“Oh OK, I’ll just have to check that with Barry, the landlord. Let me phone him and come back to you in 10 minutes.”

10 minutes later.

“Hi it’s Paul here, I’ve checked with Barry and it’s no go I’m afraid. If it were down to me, of course I’d give you a couple of days to pay, but Barry’s adamant and mentioned he has someone else interested in the room.”

It worked a treat and I never had a problem with collecting rent again.

It’s the principle of Higher Authority which puts pressure on the person you’re negotiating with without hurting the relationship you’ve built up with them. So next time you’re in negotiation and you want to pile on the pressure or say no to a compromise, invent a higher authority and refer to them before you say “no”.

Better still, create a higher authority which is a committee, so you have to run it past a collection of people. And if anyone uses it on you, ensure you agree early on who makes decisions around here. The classic decision making unit or DMU.

Thankfully house prices rebounded back up, but it wasn't until 1996 that I was able to sell the house.

The Mugging

It was 1986, late autumn, particularly dark and dismal. The Balls Pond Road in Dalston, North London, way before gentrification enveloped the area in the 1990s. As always, Dalston was heaving with people going about their business. It wasn't a wealthy area and the people matched their stereotype and the wide variety of ethnicities made the area colourful, vibrant and exciting.

The day was just any normal day in the Building Society where I worked as an Assistant Manager. We dispensed plenty of cash at the counter and in our shiny new ATM, which I was very proud of. The problem though was the only way to stock the counters and cash dispenser was from Barclays Bank, 200 yards down the road.

My duty was to walk to the bank and collect cash, bring it back for the counter and machine to consume. I dreaded it every day. The company's procedure's manual clearly stated – you must proceed to the bank in a steadfast manner, projecting an image of professionalism worthy of the society – I had to obey.

So at 2.30pm on the dot armed with my suit and a briefcase, I entered the High Street out of the branch and walked in a "steadfast" manner dodging the various characters that hung around every day.

I made it safely to the bank where I collected £8,000 in cash which I deposited in my brown leather company briefcase. The tough part of the journey was about to begin.

I didn't even see them. Two black guys appeared from nowhere; the gun was shiny, enormous and poked in my side.

The briefcase was expertly taken although I wasn't going to put up a fight, after all, would you? They disappeared down the dark alley where they came from and I darted back to the branch and called the police.

The mistake I made was to stick out like a sore thumb. No one wore suits on the Balls Pond Road and no one carried a briefcase with them either. And anyone coming out of a bank branch with a brief case might've well had a signpost on the top of their head advertising "money here, come and help yourself."

You see, in sales, you need to match your appearance with your customer, you don't want to stick out like a sore thumb, you need to match them. First impressions are made in 90 seconds and what you look like makes a huge impression, so get it right.

Thankfully the company procedure manual was changed the following week. Visits to the bank must be undertaken at different times of the day, varying your route. Cash must be put into a carrier bag matching a shop in the locality and carried under the arm. Donkey jackets are provided to hide the cash and to enable you to blend into the surrounding area.

The worst part of it all was the CID. They interviewed me and were convinced I had something to do with it, after all, why would someone lose so much cash? They followed me for the next few weeks and my bank account was tapped later as well.

Remember to look the part.

There's a Tell For Everything

Earlier this year I was invited to deliver some sales training for some clients in Dubai. It was over three days and I trained over 60 people. Nothing unusual about that, but carting 60 sets of workbooks through the skies meant I had to take 2 large suitcases with me, one completely filled with workbooks.

Naturally on my return journey I still had two large suitcases, again nothing odd there. But if you factor in that I was a businessman in a suit returning from a business trip in Dubai with two huge suitcases, it does start to look a little out of the ordinary.

The customs official at Heathrow airport thought so too and beckoned me over as I passed through customs. Here comes the suitcase search I thought, thinking about missing my train home.

He began by asking me some odd questions:

"How are you today Sir?" – Fine.

"Do these suitcases belong to you?" – Yes (obviously, since I was carrying them).

"Have you been to Dubai on business?" – Yes (obviously really since I was in a suit).

"Was it warm out there?" – Yes (obviously again, it's always warm in Dubai).

I soon figured what he was doing. He was observing me closely; looking at my physiology – body language, facial expressions – he was observing my signals when I said the word "yes". I knew what he was going to do next. He was going to do the same thing with the word "no".

"Did you manage to get any sleep?" – No (obviously – it was a daytime flight of only 6 hours).

"*Have you been doing any dangerous sports in Dubai sir?"* – No (good odds that most business meetings in Dubai don't involve bungee jumping).

"Do you have anything in those cases, that shouldn't be in there?" – No (this was the truth).

"Off you go then Sir, and sorry to trouble you". And I left.

You see he had calibrated my physiology for when I said no and was telling the truth. The body doesn't lie, there's a tell for everything and he found it for the word "*no*", so he didn't even bother to search the case. Clever man.

The police do this, so do barristers in court. I do it with my three children and I know when they're lying.

Remember physiology; there's always a tell for everything you do.

Thankfully I managed to catch my train home, it was a long arduous journey and I was keen to get the train, so thank you NLP calibration for helping me do this.

The Watch

I had just completed a one day programme for a major bank in Sheffield and, as is my volition, I was catching a train home to Cheltenham that evening. It was November, dark and moody, a sprinkle of rain in the air.

I'd arrived at the station rather stressed especially after I missed my train. Not to worry, another one was leaving in an hour, so I decided to have a little stroll along the roads surrounding the station. Sheffield was busy, it was rush hour, cars everywhere but not too many pedestrians wandering the streets, except me.

And a shadow that appeared from behind the advertising boards.

The shadow moved towards me as I walked the pavement, I slowed down. The shadow stopped and it appeared to be a young man under a large raincoat. I wasn't scared, the road was busy and well lit with street lights.

"Sorry to interrupt you sir," announced the shadow with a Cornish accent. I thought that's odd, this is Sheffield, he should be speaking in a Yorkshire twang.

"That's OK" I said moving backwards slightly.

"I'm sorry to ask this," he began "I'll get to the point. I'm a student here at Sheffield Hallam."

He did look like a student, dressed in his heavy raincoat and was about the right age.

"My dad's been taken really ill, I live in Truro, in Cornwall and I'm trying to get back to see him, but…"

Here comes the but.

"I haven't enough money for my ticket. Don't worry I'm not begging," he continued, "I noticed you're not wearing a watch, and I'm willing to sell you my watch for £40 which is the amount I need. The watch is worth over £200. My dad gave it to me for Christmas last year and he wouldn't mind."

What would you have done in the same situation?

You see, it's all about understanding and believing someone's intentions. In selling it's vital to have trust between you and your customer and sometimes we don't have long to engender trust. Trust is made up of three ingredients – competence of the salesperson, common ground between you and the customer and finally, your intentions are known.

The shadow quite clearly expressed his true intentions. It was credible – Cornish accent, student, university, we were close to the station. Watch, value and he only wanted £40. His intentions were very clear.

So in selling, make your intentions known to your customer early on, have an agenda, verbally express what you'll be doing, signpost as you continue along the buying process.

So what happened? Let me explain. I've a son at University so I said to the young man I'd buy him a ticket to get him to see his dad. I hope one day, if my son were in the same boat, someone would do the same.

We talked about his University degree. He was studying history – 19th Century political history – that was my subject at college so we spoke about Bismarck and the reunification of Germany. Fascinating.

He followed me down to the station; it was only a short walk. The ticket office queue was long and arduous so we chose the machine. I tapped Truro into the machine and asked him if he wanted a return ticket, after all I figured he probably wanted to get back to his studies at some point. I looked around to ask him again.

And he'd gone.

The Date

It was 1985, I was just 21. I was working for a small building society in Walton on Thames, I was the Assistant Manager there and expected to do the selling in the branch. Selling was still a dirty word in the mutual building society game, but the company sent me on a week-long residential sales training course. It was located somewhere in Oxford in a special training centre, I called it a mansion.

I learnt loads.

On the Friday evening after the course had finished I'd arranged a date. Her name was Caron, she worked as a receptionist at the Holiday Inn hotel in Shepperton. She was amazingly beautiful and I really wanted to make a good impression on our first date.

The course finished at lunchtime on the Friday so I drove home in my Alpha Romeo Giulietta, a lovely set of wheels housing a 1.6 litre boxer engine, it sounded great.

On my way home I thought about my date with Caron and how I could impress her. Suddenly an idea came to mind. On the course we learnt that the secret to selling and getting the customer interested was to ask questions. Find out about them, their needs, criteria and match your product to their needs.

Simple. That's what I'll do tonight.

The restaurant was a little French affair in Thames Ditton. I had rack of lamb, it was sublime. Half way through the main course, Caron stood up, pushed her chair in and said:

"Paul, you're a nice guy, but I actually don't like you."

Aghast, resembling a frog with his mouth wide open, I was speechless.

"As I said you're a nice guy, I don't like you because you ask too many questions. I feel like I'm being interrogated."

What they didn't teach me at the training course was how to sugar coat questions ensuring more of a conversation than an interrogation. I learnt afterwards that to sugar coat you use your tone of voice and you pre-frame them with permission tags such as "May I ask" or "Tell me" or "It would be interesting to know". You use plenty of verbal nods such as "Uh hur, I see, tell me more" rather than another question, and you maintain eye contact all the time.

That way it sugar coats the questions.

Too late for me. I paid the bill, the full amount by the way, fetched Caron's coat, drove her home in silence, walked her to her parents' front door and left with my tail between my legs and I never saw her ever again. And she was stunningly beautiful too. But I was only 21.

The First 5 Minutes

KAV Opening Rules OK

KAV, what's that? It's a rule for opening any presentation or training session that you're doing. We all know how important it is to get off to a great start, to engage the audience, to compel them to want to listen further.

Here's how.

KAV – kinaesthetic, auditory and visual – in that order.

Start off something that has feeling, emotion, humour – that's the kinaesthetic or kino start. Use a story that explains who you are. I have a couple of favourites I use that really show who I am, have humour, and contain emotion.

Maybe humour – something funny in the news might do – don't tell jokes. Something funny that happened to you on the way in. Emotion, sentiment, passion.

Then comes auditory; lower your voice, make it resonant, bring in vocal variety – people want to hear your voice next to really connect and then finally comes…

Visual; in a picture on screen or image painted in their minds.

KAV rules OK. Next time you're planning a presentation or training session, use the KAV start.

The 90:90 Rule

She couldn't do anything wrong, she was loved by millions, a perfect embodiment of the 90:90 rule. She also made mistakes, but we forgave her.

He was also adored by millions, a trusted sportsman and great evangelist. Again, he made some mistakes, but the world forgave him. Another incarnation of the 90:90 rule.

The 90:90 rule is very simple yet profound and will have an immediate and impactful effect on your selling and coaching.

In the first 90 seconds of meeting someone, or seeing them on TV, we make up an impression of that person. We've known this for, like, ever. We often forget that 90% of this first impression lasts forever, whatever goes on in the future. It's called the 90:90 rule. In the first 90 seconds of meeting someone, you make a lasting impression that will remain intact by 90%.

This makes the whole concept of first impressions so much more vital. So how do you carry yourself off in the first 90 seconds? How do you walk, instigate the handshake, break the ice, smile, match body language and energy, engage eye contact? What are you wearing, are you shoes clean, what about your car outside the client's offices? After all, visitor spots are always close to the entrance and people have been known to peer outside their window to watch you – so assume that they are.

If the first 90 seconds worked well, then the customer will place a neat halo over your head and you will get away with the odd mistake or two. However, if you blew it, you'll have a perpetual pair of horns instead. Not good for business generation.

I first saw her on my grainy black and white TV in 1981 when she looked down at the camera and slowly raised her eyes in such an innocent shy manner. And for him, it was 1971 when he first spoke about race relations. Princess Diana and Mohammed Ali.

Now I Know My ABC...D

Next time will you sing with me?

I used to love watching Sesame Street as a kid. It was an American TV show with Muppet style puppets. Every episode had some major learning point for us kids but we loved the programme for its colour, fun and songs.

One of my favourite songs was the ABC song which ended; "Now I know my ABC, next time will you sing with me?"

Now this song always reminds me of the ABCD of presentations. A really clever mnemonic to help you with the first few minutes of any presentation to get it off to the right start and give you lots of confidence to continue.

1. A – Attention
2. B – Benefits
3. C – Credibility
4. D - Direction

Attention

"Unaccustomed as I am to public speaking...."

"Hello, my name is Paul Archer..."

"Uhm, OK, let's get started then shall we?"

What do these three have in common? Yes, of course - they are bland, listless and terribly unexciting presentation starters.

Your first priority is to get the attention of your audience, especially if you are selling and presenting at the same time. We don't have the luxury of time, so we need to grab their attention in the first few moments.

Now it helps if you've done your circulating with the audience beforehand and have done some homework on the people sitting in front of you. This gives you some pointers as to the type of attention getter to use.

I'm not saying you should tell a joke. Perhaps you could but make sure it's a self effacing joke to show your humility and not embarrass anyone sitting down.

- Share a quotation. You can get thousands of these from the Internet and one might fit the bill.
- Tell a story or metaphor which will link into the main points.
- Ask a searching question.
- A call to action.
- This day in history.

Benefits

Once you have their attention, tease them with some of the main benefits or the major one benefit they will get from listening and maybe taking action.

It might be obvious to you, but we have to think of our audience. WIIFM? What's in it for me? Think in their shoes and share some benefits.

"What I'd like to do is to give you some bang up to date pointers which will help you decide your direction over the next year. These could give you a competitive advantage."

Enough to intrigue, excite, and make people want to listen more.

Credibility

It's important to get this part done, if the audience has never met you before. Sometimes, in more formal settings, the Master of Ceremonies will introduce you and help to build your credibility.

However in most business presentations, particularly sales pitches or "beauty parades", you really do have to cement your credibility. Don't overdo this bit. Don't fall into the trap of telling them all about you, your history, and your qualifications.

That's zzz time.

Instead use a reassurance statement. This statement should include your name and your experience, both in the customer's industry or sector and your experience in dealing with similar problems to your customer.

"My name is Paul Archer; I've been working with salespeople across the globe for almost 20 years helping them to earn their bonuses. For the last two years I've been helping businesses like yours get better closing ratios from their Key Accounts."

Direction

I love taking my three children on car journeys. My wife and I have a bet as to when the first one will ask "Are we there yet Dad?" Normally my wife wins. So I reply "Not yet Euan, we've just passed Winchester and we'll probably be at Nana's in half an hour."

And they're happy for the next few miles.

Now someone gave me a brilliant tip the other week to help in this arduous purpose. Keep telling them where you are and how long there is to go.

"Hey guys, we've just passed Stonehenge. Can you see it on your right? And we'll be at Nana's in 20 minutes, in time for an ice cream."

Since that piece of advice, we've never looked back and you can use the same idea in your presentations.

Tell your audience where you're going to take them. Give them clear direction. Not an agenda, these are for books. Presentations need signposts which tell you where you're going. At each junction the audience needs reminding where they've come from and then where they're going to go next.

The best analogy is one of those property purchase programmes on the TV. My favourite is Phil and Kirsty doing "Location, Location, Location". Just as they're coming up to a commercial break, Kirsty will quickly recap the main points covered so far and give one or two tempters of what you'll see after the break. This not only gives you clear direction, but tempts you to come back after the break.

And when you return from the break, Phil takes over and reminds you what they did before the break and then tempts you further with the major benefits of the next 15 minutes.

Brilliant stuff and certainly worth repeating in your presentations.

So give direction and then constantly signpost your way to the end. And as you approach the end signal that the end is in sight, summarise each of your key points, remember the power of three – three major points maximum. Invite questions; never ever finish on a Q&A because if there are no questions, you'll go out like a damp squib.

Invite questions, deal with these and then restate your aim and purpose and end with a call to action.

With the end in sight:

- Signal that the end is in sight
- Summarise each of your key points
- Invite questions: don't end on Q&A
- Restate the aim and overall purpose
- Definite finishes – call to action

And now you know your ABC…and D, next time will you sing with me…?

How to be Introduced

Being introduced properly is an essential ingredient to a successful talk. A solid intro sets the scene and gets the audience on your side before you start. Plus you get a recommendation from the Chairperson, this is worth its weight in gold.

Use the TIS technique. T – Topic; I – Interest; S – Speaker.

Let me explain.

Topic

Introduce just the topic to start with. Tell the audience a little about the content or share the problem that's going to be solved.

"Our final presentation today looks at the perennial challenge of motivation to get the best out of our sales teams."

Interest

Now the opportunity comes about to generate some interest. Perhaps pose a problem you know the audience might have, and promise some answers. Remember WIIFM – what's in it for me? Your audience are very selfish in that they want some benefits.

"You know how difficult it is to motivate your sales team all the time, well our next speaker is going to share some fabulous techniques to help you do this."

Speaker

Now comes the speaker's details. Build their credibility.

"Please welcome our 7 times published author and renowned expert on the topic of motivation…Mike Hammersmith."

And let's hope Mike Hammersmith lives up to our expectation.

Name, Rank and Serial Number

I was watching a remake of the Colditz TV Series at the weekend on Gold Channel and the Allied prisoner was being interrogated by the Germans. At every request the prisoner would say only his *"name, rank and serial number",* much to the German soldier's angst.

And in the same way, I hear many business presentations starting with the same routine: Name, rank and serial number.

"My name is Paul Archer, I'm the CEO of Archer Training Ltd and I've 14 years experience on this topic."

Dullsville.com.

And some even have these credentials stamped on the first page of their PowerPoint deck.

Don't do it, it's boring, uneventful and plain uninspiring.

Bear in mind you have only about 10 seconds to capture their attention. Perhaps you could come in with something more inspiring:

"Today I'm going to excite you, entice you and tickle your taste buds. Let's look at the latest ideas from our company that might help you in 2017."

Sounds better than *"I'm Bert Bacharach, Sales Director at MC Enterprises, I've been with MC for 5 years, and been in this sector for 14."*

Charge up Your Energy Bank Account

It takes plenty of energy to speak in public and your audience deserves you to be on top of your game when presenting. The trick is to charge up your energy bank account before you speak.

Here are some ideas to ensure you have a full tank of energy:

- The usual culprits such as exercise and a good night's sleep work wonders. Ear plugs and hotel bedrooms work well together especially if you're a light sleeper.
- Feed off the audience's energy, with some involvement or interaction. This will boost you incredibly.
- Start off your presentation with lots of high energy. My motto is "You're 'aving it large."
- Tap up an anchor to ignite a state of high energy. My favourite is music. I've a CD burnt in my car, with a number of tracks which anchor high energy for me:
- Good Morning Britain – Aztec Camera
- Bohemian Rhapsody - Queen

- Ride my See Saw – The Moody Blues
- Champagne Supernova – Oasis
- Common People – Pulp
- Torn – Natalie Imbruglia
- Love Vigilantes – New Order
- Mr Brightside – The Killers
- Jimmy Jimmy – The Undertones
- King of the Kerb – Echobelly
- Nothing in my Way – Keane
- Survival – Muse
- Electricity – OMD
- Spitting Games – Snow Patrol
- The Raven – The Stranglers
- School – Supertramp
- Whiskey in the Jar – Thin Lizzy
- Something in the Air – Thunderclap Newman
- Road – Trees
- Eat That Up, It's Good For You – Two Door Cinema Club
- Queen Bitch – David Bowie

These are unique to me, they bring back memories or a state of high energy. You probably have your own, but you're welcome to borrow my playlist.

High energy speaking – your audience deserves it.

Make the Room Work for You

Tips on Arrival

Always, always, arrive in plenty of time for your appearance on stage. Ideally, visit the venue in advance so that you can have a look at the room, and most importantly, get a "feel" for the position you will be working from. Go up on stage (or to the front of the room if there is no stage), close your eyes and imagine the audience giving you a huge round of applause. This visualisation will help reduce your nervousness when your time comes.

Other things you should do in advance when you "work the room" -

- Check your path from where you are sitting to where you will be standing (look for cables, carpet edges).
- Rehearse your walk to the stage.
- Talk to the technician and run a sound check.
- Find out if the speaker before you is using equipment that needs to be removed or switched.
- Walk the stage and get comfortable.
- Find out how the microphone switches on and off.
- Make sure you hand your introduction to the MC.
- Ask for the stage lights to be put on, and check that you're happy with them.
- Check your call time.

- Find out who is managing the event, and how to contact them.

One more thing - if you don't like the layout of the room, ask if you can change it. For example, I hate to speak in a hall with an aisle down the centre. If the chairs are moveable, I always ask for the aisle to be closed. On every occasion but one (when the manager was paranoid about evacuating in case of fire), the venue was happy to help. So just ask.

Let the Lectern Languish

Haydock Park – 2016. I was presenting that morning for 45 minutes and as is my volition, I was working with the sound team to ensure my visuals and the microphone would work without a hitch. This team can make or break your talk so they're important allies.

I looked up at the stage and someone had put an enormous bright white wooden lectern on the stage. Without thinking I blurted out "Who's put that monstrosity on the stage?"

"I did" defended the head technician. "Whoops" I thought as I imagined my microphone going off half way through my presentation.

"The client asked me to bring one along, I've just bought it."

I quickly had to justify my reaction. Here's how:

- Standing behind the lectern restricts the speaker's ability to use their body language and gestures to support the message.
- The lectern acts a barrier.
- It encourages the speaker to read notes as they are in front of them. Disaster.

- They stifle any energy from the speaker.
- Often the audience has anchored any speaker that stands behind the lectern as a dull listless speaker, since every speaker before them was so.
- They're not bullet proof, by the way, although some nervous speakers thought they were.

"It's not my fault" said my technician buddy, "I don't like them, I was told to bring it by the organiser."

Let the lectern be banished from the kingdom of the event organiser.

Room Mechanics

Thank goodness I arrived the afternoon before. I was hired as a speaker coach to help the annual convention flow swimmingly, they had some managers who had been asked at the last minute to present to the sales force and were, understandably, shaking with nerves.

That was the easy part. On my arrival, it was turmoil; chairs were being laid out by the hotel staff, the stage was being erected. The smallest screen possible was being set up. At least there were professional audio visual people turning up later that night.

"Can you help us please Paul, you've done lots of these things, can you give us some guidance about setting up the room?" Of course I agreed, putting the coaching off for a couple of hours.

Once the stage was erected, the first thing I did was grab the organiser and stand alongside her on the stage, looking around at the room. I gazed around the room taking it all in imagining where the 100 people would be seated and how much of the stage and screen they could see.

Elvis and Stagecraft

During a lull in this year's Christmas celebrations, my family watched footage of Elvis Presley performing in Las Vegas in the early 1970s. It was possibly his most efficacious period.

"It's all in his movement", we all concluded and if you watch Elvis perform, he does boss the stage, every movement choreographed to perfection.

How should you "boss" the stage when presenting? There are a number of rules that you should adopt:

- Don't pace up and down, left to right – it's a sign of nerves. You may not be nervous; the movement might be habitual but the audience will see through it and think you're less than capable.
- Move only for a reason.
- Move when you change topic. For example, when you want to make a point or tell a story, or just address another part of the audience.
- Many speakers, myself included, use the theatre stage conventions. Here you have five positions which I've drawn for you on the next page:

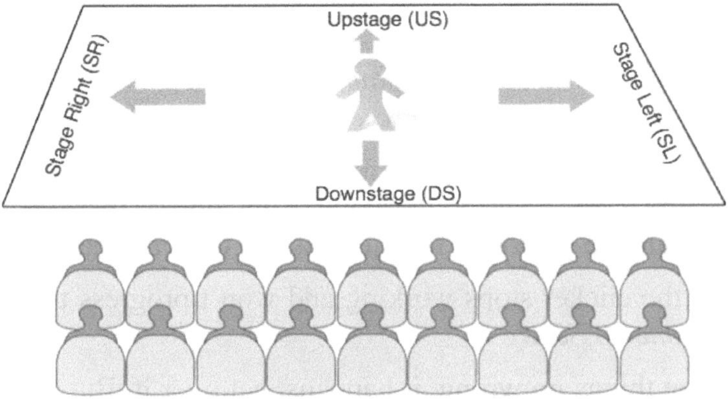

- I generally use down stage centre to make an important point, maybe the phrase that pays when telling a story. I mostly stand in centre stage, rarely in up stage, unless I want the audience to ponder over something.
- Stage left and right can be anchored to a story, usually on centre stage left and when showing PowerPoint, I stand at centre stage right (because most audiences read from their left to right). There's a whole lot of science behind all of this.
- Remember the phrase "take centre stage"? That's where it comes from.
- Dissolve, bomb, cut down with an axe, the lectern and never stand behind it. They're not bullet proof.

The film clip of Suspicious Minds is a masterclass in using the stage, it's here on YouTube if you care to watch it https://youtu.be/Wb0Jmy-JYbA. But whatever you do, don't do the Elvis Knee; that's not a good look in a business presentation.

You Hear a Loud Crash

"Do you know this place is haunted, and the ghosts like to turn off the visuals whenever a presentation is going well?"

I heard this from a speaker friend of mine, Neil Dickey, and it made me laugh. The PowerPoint went down, there were no visuals and he got away with it, with the clever remark.

When the clicker stops working and won't progress the slides. "*Beam me up Scotty.*"

You see things go wrong, it happens, get over it. But have pre-planned comedy to help the audience laugh it off since they're as embarrassed as you.

Someone's phone goes off even though the organiser or you have pleaded earlier for them to be silenced. *"Time for your pill"* is a little edgy, but it does get a laugh.

- You hear a loud crash outside, *"I always like to start my talk with a bang."*
- You trip on the steps to the stage, "*I also do magic tricks.*"
- The flipchart pen is dry as a bone, *"I wish I extended the warranty on this pen."*
- You just can't find the handout amongst the sheets, *"Just give me an hour, I'll find it."*
- The projector light goes out, "*Hello, wakey wakey, is anyone in there?*"
- The lights go out in the room, *"I hope my presentation hasn't left you in the dark.*"

- You get loud feedback on the mike, *"This is the result of many years of inhaling helium balloons."*
- You drop the clicker or microphone, *"If it wasn't for gravity, that wouldn't have happened."*
- Something is broken, "*I know it's time for a break, but this is ridiculous.*"

The Scourge of the Smartphone

I read recently of a cinema chain in the USA, AMC which owns 400 screens, has converted the back row to "texting aisles" where cinema goers can text and Facebook away without disturbing other viewers.

For me, watching a blockbuster at the movies, gripped to your seat, is an experience which can easily be disturbed with the flash of a smartphone screen, but this cinema chain has decided to ride with it.

The axiom is *"if you can't beat them, join them"* and this is exactly how we should treat texters or smartphone addicts on our courses. Don't try and beat them, we never will, people regard their phones as third limbs and get all shaky and sweaty when we take them away.

On courses, meetings and workshops, do you fight them or join them?

If you fight them, you:

- Ban phones.
- Ask them to switch them off.
- Tut tut when people start texting.

- Get really annoyed when someone uses one while you're presenting.

If you join them, you:

- Welcome smartphones.
- Actively allow their use.
- Channel their use to the meeting's objectives.
- Run quizzes using phones.
- Use them as microphones for the Q&A – yes, you can get software for that.
- Use them to poll the audience.
- Set up a hashtag to encourage comments and questions.
- Set exercises that ask them to google something or look something up.
- Pick a YouTube video for them to watch which helps with the workshop.
- Have five minute email breaks.
- Make your workshop far more involved so you don't find yourself lecturing all the time.

So are you trying to beat them or are you joining them? I'm not sure about the back row of the cinema being used for texting; I thought it had other uses.

The Body Language of Public Speaking

Next time you watch a politician on TV speaking to an audience, turn the volume down and watch. Then interpret what is being said just by observing the body language. Try it – it's amazing what you read into the message just by watching the person speaking.

How many of you have made your mind up about a speaker's message without concerning yourself about the words, purely by observation and your intuition? And this is going on right now somewhere in the world. A business speaker has a good message but it's being clouded by the way it's presented.

The purpose of this eBook is to remind you, no, convince you of some key steps to take to ensure your body doesn't cloud the message next time you get up to speak.

Let's kick off with the body language and work around the body reminding ourselves of what to do. We'll then cover movement around your stage.

The Head

My daughter has just started playgroup and she brought home a picture of Daddy. An amazing picture showing Daddy with a large smiling face and 2 arms and legs. However the body was missing. This happened with my sons when they first went to playgroup.

Inquisitive as ever, I asked the nursery teacher why Bethan had missed out the body. "Children of that age don't focus on the body, they are only concerned with the face and that's all they see. That's why clowns paint their faces so brightly and children love them."

As adults, we still have childish habits and one of them is to focus on the face of someone who is speaking to you. So get those expressions working for you and really exaggerate the meaning. Smile, frown, look angry, shocked, amazed – but please always be congruent with your message.

Eye Contact

Next we have eye contact. This is probably the one skill, when mastered, that does the most to engage the audience and build trust and rapport with the audience. The rule is to hardly ever let go. Imagine you're playing tennis or squash: you never let your eye off the ball otherwise you'll miss a shot. Likewise, keep your eye contact on the audience at all times.

Careful with the lighthouse technique as well – this is where speakers sweep the audience in a repetitive swishing motion that does more to put people to sleep than engage.

It always reminds me of those old Second World War POW escape movies when the escapees are nudging their way out of the tunnel, dodging the sweeping searchlights. As soon as the light has moved along its repetitive motion, they dash to safety. In a similar way, your audience will escape you when your sweeping leaves them.

Instead have a conversation with your audience with your eyes. Randomly contact with each audience member and give them 2 to 3 seconds of eye contact and move onto the next person. Maintain this random movement. Find those in the audience who like just a little more eye contact and be aware of those who want slightly less.

When faced with a large audience – I mean more than 25 or so people, adopt a similar habit but don't give each person eye contact. That'll take ages. Instead, clump people into small groups and give these clumps the same eye contact as if they were one person. I tell you, that because of the distance between you and a large audience, this gives people the impression that you are looking at them.

Feet

Now let's go to the other extreme of your body: your feet and legs. Now what do you do with these limbs? Not a lot really unless you are moving around your stage, that's movement with a purpose, not aimless wandering that only distracts the audience.

Do you remember your mother asking you to stand up straight? Maybe and it really was good advice. Try to stand with both feet firmly on the ground pretty much the same distance apart as your shoulders. Keep them balanced so your body is not leaning to one side. Don't look like a cat walk model or if you're supping a pint at the bar of your local. Stand straight and look professional, not a slouch.

Nerves…that's a word that conjures up fear and dread every time people stand up and speak in public. And sure enough you'll have nerves. Professionals call it adrenaline and you need that to do a really good job. If you don't have nerves or adrenaline, you might as well not bother because you can't be bothered. So welcome nerves, call them adrenaline and make them work for you.

Nerves will show in the periphery of your body. The ends such as feet, hands, head. Keeping your feet still transfers this energy to the top part of your body where it should go.

Now I didn't say you should stay rigid to the spot; that would be terrible for 20 minutes. Instead, focus your attention on preventing aimless movement, pacing up and down, shifting from side to side. Keep well balanced and professional.

The Body

Next we have the trunk. That's the bit my daughter missed out. Not much you can do with the trunk apart from keeping it straight. Not like the Sergeant Major on the parade ground but not slouched either. Relaxed and comfortable. The worst sin is to block the invisible mid line that runs from between your 2 feet and your head. Block it and you place a barrier with your audience. Just don't block it – that's the rule.

Hands and Arms

Next the arms and hands. I've spoken with hundreds of people who honestly don't know what to do with their hands.

Shame really, so they copy people on the TV, especially weather girls: they grasp their hands together. I've never understood this although I was guilty myself once. It made me feel better and comfortable so much that as soon as I stood up to talk, my two hands came together. And when I got really nervous I used to rub them together too. Someone told me I looked like a market trader making lots of money. That sure went down well with my audiences.

So what do you do with them? Behind your back, but that just reminds me of Prince Charles. In your pockets, I hear you say. No, you're hiding something, keeping back from the audience and besides, you're missing out on a great weapon. No, the answer is to use them to back up your message by gesturing.

I did some training work in the Netherlands earlier this year for an international food company. The delegates were from all over Europe – Spain, Italy, Germany, Netherlands, France…I watched each one present on many occasions and it was so great to watch those from Mediterranean countries who naturally speak with their hands. They gesture so well and when given the go ahead to gesture during their speeches, they really went for it. Us Anglo Saxons are the stilted ones and we need to learn to speak with our hands.

I'm a big Glastonbury Festival fan and when I'm watching the bands playing on stage I'm a fair distance away. The gestures from the lead singer will be dramatic. If he wants us to clap, he won't politely pat his hands together, he'll launch them over his head to make a very dramatic clap.

This is how we should gesture with audiences. Large dramatic gestures to help the audience understand what you're saying. Broad gestures that welcome every person into your speech, building rapport. Think of your speech content and let your hands do the talking. Watch deaf people doing their sign language – it really is a very clever way of finding your gesture buttons.

And when not gesturing, or talking, maybe standing still to take questions from your audience, assume the assertive stance. Standing straight with your arms and hands down by your sides, in a relaxed assertive and confident manner.

Body Movement

Finally, body movement. Movement can be an enormously effective way of engaging the audience into your message. Clean your stage – remove obstacles, tape wires to the floor, so you don't trip over them, place the screen to the side.

Yes, to the side and I wish more meeting planners would situate their screen to the right or left of the audience and not bang in the middle. You've probably been there or seen it. The slides are beaming onto the screen, the table is full of people, so to let the person on your left see the screen, you move into the corner of the room. You're lost, you're gone – you've lost eye contact with the audience who are busy reading the slides.

If you're able to position the screen to the left or right of the audience, you'll be able to remain in the centre of the stage. Trust what is on your slides and be aware of reading directly from the screen – this takes your eye contact away from the audience and is a cardinal sin. Have a laptop screen in front of you or learn your slides. Better still use fewer of them, but that's another story.

Once you have a clear space, do move around with a purpose. I've used past, present and future by gradually moving along an imaginary line. The audience can see the time moving along as well as hear. I've used one side of the stage for the advantages of an idea I'm promoting, and the other side for the disadvantages. I've placed flipcharts at both sides of the room to mirror these place anchors.

Move forward towards your audience when you want to make a really big point. Move backwards when you want them to reflect on something. Move to your left or right to change the subject or pace of your delivery.

Do move around your stage, but with a distinct purpose.

The next time you're observing and listening to a speaker, try and cut out the sound and focus entirely on the visual aspects. Try and interpret what he or she is saying just by the body language alone. You may not be right in your assumption of the meaning, but it's the impression that everyone else is probably getting too. And first impressions last for ages.

The Roof Garden

The 13th floor of the Radisson Blu in Dubai. I'd arrived that morning from London and I was presenting the following morning. Being November in the UK, I was keen to experience the warmth and sunshine of the outdoor pool on the top floor.

And I wasn't disappointed; radiant sunshine and a lush view of the city.

I wandered over the edge of the poolside and chose a sun bed, resting my book and sun glasses on the table, I slowly lowered my British frame onto the bed and lay down to savour the sunshine.

Shortly a waiter arrived, who spoke perfect English and engaged me in a conversation.

"How was your flight?"

"Fine, thank you for asking."

"You're a pilot with the British Airways party aren't you?"

"No, I'm merely their passenger, what makes you think I'm a pilot?"

"Because of the way you walked across the poolside and settled down, you looked like a pilot."

Now you can imagine my smile. Like a Cheshire cat was I, completely complimented. I purred.

On a sober note, we know about first impressions and your arrival into the client's premises, walking over to your customer in the lobby is the first impression they see. Walk like James Bond I call it.

1. Work out your route before you start walking.
2. Walk slowly, no jerky movements, firm strides.
3. Hold your head high and lock on eye contact with your customer.
4. Sway your arms by your sides, no touching of the body or face and don't keep anything in front of you like a folder.
5. If you have a case, hold it in your left hand because you shake with your right, sweaty palms and all that.
6. If you're walking through a crowd, use your arms as imaginary indicators to show your direction of travel, people will respond.
7. Smile as you walk, smiling is engaging.

And you'll appear to be like James Bond and give a great first impression.

He was my new friend on the top floor pool. He probably uses the airline pilot line with all the men, if truth be told, but it sounded nice on that sublime afternoon.

Owning the Stage with Your Voice

Trains, Planes and Automobiles

One of my all time favourite movies is Trains, Planes and Automobiles starring Steve Martin and John Candy as two hapless travellers trying to get home for Christmas. It's a hoot but when I'm on trains and planes, there's one thing I'll instantly do and that's snooze. There's something soporific about the steady shunting of a train or the hum within an aircraft. That dull monotonous tone that's more effective than sleeping pills.

In the same manner, speakers who use a dull, monotonous voice will put their audience to sleep and you don't want to do that. Here are some tips to ensure your voice captivates and vitalises the audience:

- Pace. This is the first aspect to get right. New speakers tend to speak at the same pace as they talk naturally; around 180 to 200 words a minute. This is a mistake as speakers should slow down to around 120 to 150 words a minute. Once you've mastered this, then you can start to vary your pace to add effect. For example a sudden increase in pace indicates excitement or a thrill, maybe the culmination of your story. Slowing your pace down deliberately emphasises an important point and oddly, whispering draws attention to what you are saying almost like a secret is being divulged. Only do this if you have a microphone though.
- Pitch. This is your voice going up and down. Deep baritone just like Barry White or high pitch falsetto like

Barry Gibb. There are 5 to 8 available notes, professional singers can access them all. I can access just 4 and have a male voice box so can't go too high. The secret is to vary the pitch to interest the audience but not to sound like a children's TV presenter. Do any of you remember the pitch used by the football results reporters in the 1980s? They'd mastered it.

- Volume. There's a difference between volume and projection. I focus more on my projection than simply speaking louder. You can achieve this by raising your head slightly, but don't start looking down your nose at people – we stopped that when the British Aristocracy faded away. Open your mouth more; practise this. The best practise method is to say to yourself EO, EO, EO as many times as you can. Don't do this in front of people though, they'll think you're a donkey, and you don't want that, do you?

- Resonance. Next time you listen to a newsreader on the radio, listen out for their resonance. Both males and females can do this, males have a deeper one of course. Resonance is very attractive to the ear and can be practised. Learn to hum to yourself before speaking but again, don't do this in front of people, they'll think you're chanting to the Guru.

- Emphasis and intonation. Emphasising certain words can be tempting to attract attention to a major point, as can dropping your voice at the end of the sentence. This ensures the audience accepts it as a sign of authority. The football reporters would do this in the 1980s. Down if the team lost, up if they won. Liverpool 1 (voice down): Manchester United 2 (up), although that never happened in the 1980s as Liverpool won every time.

Trains, planes and automobiles – places to snooze but don't sleep in a car unless you're the passenger. And refrain from putting your audience to sleep with your presentations, that's just plain rude.

4 Voice Exercises

The following exercises should be done regularly in order to gain the benefits.

Resonance

A resonant voice gives you depth and authority alongside a richer voice. It ticks all the box of the modern professional expert who wishes to gain credibility quickly. Here's how to develop a resonant voice:

1. Stand or sit, but hold your posture well.
2. Choose a note to hum.
3. Next hum it for an entire breath.
4. Go low with your humming.
5. Feel the vibration in your chest, learn to recognise the signs of a resonant voice.
6. Repeat over again.

Clarity and mouth control

Useful for fluency and expressions.

1. Stand or sit but hold your posture well.

2. Say a letter out loud as clearly as you can, for about 10 seconds, or your breath runs out.
3. Move your whole mouth and accentuate your cheek muscles.
4. Now do the rest of the alphabet in the same manner.
5. Repeat the alphabet.

Quick clarity

This is a quick exercise to do when you haven't much time.

1. Say the letters QEQR.
2. Move your whole mouth and accentuate your cheek muscles.

Developing intonation

1. If you have children, read a character book and put on some accents.
2. If you don't have children, grab a company brochure and read it as though you were talking to a child. Make it interesting.

How to Use the Microphone

What must you never do when you visit the bathroom or drink fizzy water? Use a microphone or forget to switch it off, which we've all done before.

Microphones have an amazing ability to amplify your voice and allow you to speak for prolonged periods without damaging or over stretching your voice.

Typically, you'd need one when you start addressing audiences of 25 plus, although you can enjoy voice training that would allow you to project to larger audiences without one, but this is tiring.

Here are some tips on how to handle the mike:

- Microphones come in three guises – lapel, hand-held and lectern attached. If holding a mike, place it in your left hand and use your dominant hand for gestures. Keep it about a hand's length from your mouth.
- When using a lapel mike, attach it to your jacket or shirt. Have the mike at a hands' length away from your mouth. Stretch out your hands, line the thumb with your mouth and position the mike where your little finger is.
- Test it's on by tapping the mike with your finger and hear the soft thud from the speakers. Don't do "testing, testing, one, two, three". You do that with the sound engineers before your audience arrives.
- Mikes should be your best buddies since they can make you sound like Elvis Presley, if they want to, and if they don't like you, they'll make you sound like Donald Duck.
- When testing, walk as close to the speakers as you can before you get the feedback. Then map out the stage in your head as to where you can move to without that blackboard screeching sound, that's just horrible.
- Ensure you have new batteries in the radio receiver, these things consume batteries in minutes.
- And switch off the receiver once you've finished and before you visit the bathroom.

If you didn't figure out the fizzy water warning, this will make you burp uncontrollably and that sounds like an earthquake with a microphone.

How to Focus on Your Audience

Are you a PowerPoint Gazer?

In the early 1990s, a music genre called shoe gazers began and as you've guessed it, the guitarists would play whilst staring at their shoes. They looked odd but the music they produced was terrific.

Shoe gazers launched the success of many Britpop and Indie bands, my favourite bands were Suede, Echobelly and Elastica.

Enough of the music reminiscing.

Whiz forward in time and we have a new genre; not in music, but for business presenters called PowerPoint gazers – presenters who constantly gaze at their PowerPoint slides because these remind them on what to talk about. They don't know their material well enough or haven't taken steps to prepare their content.

This makes them too content focused as they spend brain power thinking and remembering what to say. It takes their attention away from their audience.

Dangerous.

I know why, so do you. Because we're busy and can't find the time to prepare. However we need to master our content if we're to honour our audience – if we don't, we're not caring for our paid audience. Remember audiences pay with their precious time, not just money.

Allow me to offer you some tips and strategies which I've gleaned after professionally presenting for over 20 years.

I'm going to start with how you can create prompts and notes, then how to practise and memorise your speech and finally, on the day of the presentation, how to keep on track with your content.

All allowing you to focus exclusively on your audience and not become a PowerPoint Gazer.

Prompts and Notes

My first training team that was weaned in the early 1990s, as shoe gazers became of age, were all successful salespeople who I plucked from the field sales force to become excellent trainers. Our challenge was to help them stay audience focused whilst presenting top drawer content. I began by teaching them how to make notes that they could refer to during the sessions so to keep on track and remember the key points required. For Christmas I bought them plastic recipe book stands to house their notes with one aim:

So they could glance at the notes during their session without taking their eyes off their most precious resource – the audience – but still know what to talk about.

And I recommended 3 varieties of notes – mindmaps, bullets on cards and the A4 sheets that PowerPoint produces for notes. All these were placed on the recipe stand.

Mindmaps

I'm sure you've come across mindmaps before and maybe you create them regularly. I do for a variety of purposes and one is for notes whilst I'm running talks and presentations. Here's an example of a Key Note on the topic of NLP in selling:

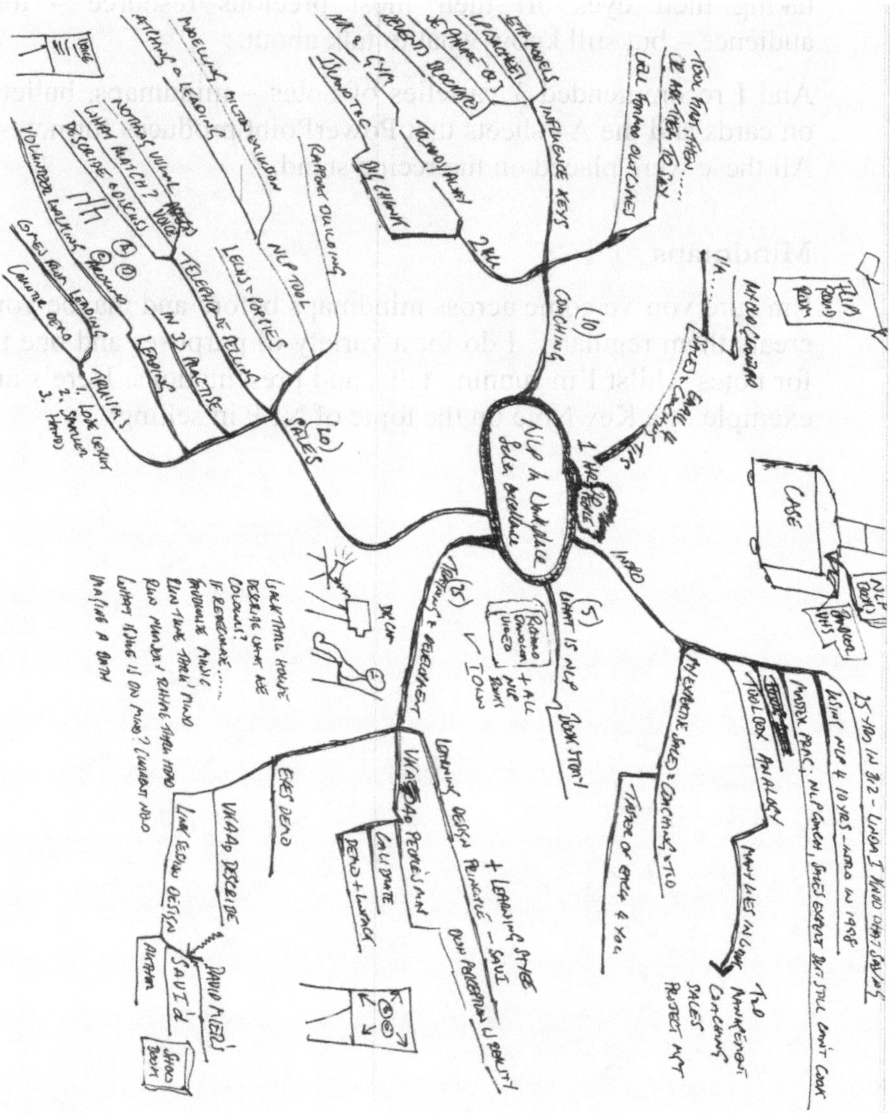
NLP in Workplace Sales Excellence
SALES
COACHING
INTRO
CASE
WHAT IS NLP
INFLUENCE KEYS
TOOLBOX ANALOGY

This stays at the front of my presentation on my recipe book stand to enable me to glance and remember the section I was talking about. Maybe you could create one of these to remind you of what to say. I like to use colour and pictures to help me remember parts of my trainings and talks. The trick is to glance at the notes when needed, not to stop and read them half way through – that's amateurish.

Bullets

Bullets are summarised points i.e. short one or two words describing the content of your talk. A series of bullets can summarise a whole 1 hour talk or a 7 hour seminar. Each bulleted word should spark your brain to recall a series of information, points and stories to enable you to present that area of your talk. That's all that is needed if you have put your time into preparing the content.

Your bullets can look as you like them to look, but they must be glance'able from a distance of 3 feet or one metre, so make the font size large enough to see at a distance.

There's an example on the next page which is, again, a Key Note on the same topic as the mindmap earlier.

INTERPRET YOUR PREFERENCE
HOW RECOGNISE; THEN USES
NUMBER OF WAYS - DETAILED
PHYSIOLOGY
FOVEAL V PERIPHERAL
SYNCING & PERRY VIDEO
COUPLE IN RESTAURANT
MX SPINONE'S
ACCELERATE CONNECTION
PAIR EXERCISE - QUICK
VOICE POSITION

LEWIS & POPPIES
COMMON GROUND
KNOW THIS
MORE SUBTLE
NLP & JABS
SEE WORLD THRU OUR EYES
WRONG!
SEE THROUGH CLIENT
COMMS MODEL
USE CLIENT, STAFF, PHONE

DEMONSTRATE
PAIR EXERCISE - QUICK
VOCAL TYPE
EXERCISE IN PAIRS
WORDS/PHRASES USED
EXERCISE - POSITIONING X 4'S
LETS EXAMINE COMMS TECHNIQUES
V - A - K - D - SLIDES
TESTING THE WATER
POLICE STORY & CALIBRATION

INFLUENCE & COMMUNICATE
QUESTIONNAIRE FIRST
DON'T INTERPRET YET!
DESCRIBE VAKD
VISUAL - RUGBY & GENT'S
AUDITORY - AGASSI & SAMPRA
KINO - CLINTON HANDSHAKE
- THOUGHTS WEIGHING
HEAVY ON MIND
DIGITAL - ANDROID & ALGO

PowerPoint Notes

PowerPoint provides its own note page, you may have seen it. It helps you to print out the slides with your own notes underneath the slide. These work so long as you keep the notes you make brief enough and large to be able to read them using the 3 foot rule.

The major problem with this method is you end up with a collection of sheets of paper which can look clumsy and awkward when presenting. I've seen speakers use these when presenting from the dreaded podium and very few use them well, as they have a tendency to type lots of notes and practically read these to the audience. That's a lack of preparation.

They are useful for preparing and practising your talk though.

Political speakers and Heads of Business are trained to read these in their presentations but they are weaned off reading them through and trained to capture a sentence or two by looking down, they then look up to engage the audience or camera and say their words. They repeat this process all the way through.

Practise Before the Event

I don't need to tell you that the more practice you do, the better your presentation. It relieves nerves, makes you more audience centred, allows you to adlib on the day and come over more polished and professional.

The problem is time, or lack of it, especially if you work in a corporate environment.

My advice is to use your down-time to practise. Create your talk first and transfer it to notes, cards or mindmaps – something to remind you. Make sure you're comfortable with the content and can carry your notes with you. Then you use downtime to read out your talk and glance at your notes to remind you. Carry a master copy of the speech or slides.

But if it provides solace for you, many speakers miss out large chunks of the content and the audience still gets the message.

Read your speech out loud in:

- The car.
- Whilst walking the dog.
- Out running.
- In the shower (but don't take your notes in with you. The shower is the best place to memorise the first 5 minutes of your talk. Yes, you need to do this).
- On the plane (but read to yourself).
- In the gym.
- Waiting for the kids at the school gates.
- Whilst cooking the dinner.
- Doing the housework.
- The list goes on.

Future Pacing the Talk

Once you've nailed the talk, consider future pacing your presentation. This is a splendid way of relieving nerves and creating bucket loads of confidence. It firms up your timings as well and allows you to immediately connect with your audience when you arrive, because you've practised.

I've been known to future pace my entire presentation of 45 minutes by visualising where I am, the audience reactions, the use of slides, my interactive exercises, questions from the audience, particularly the Q&A.

It's what I do for a living so I make the time, but I do appreciate some of you reading this may not be able to find this precious resource, so try speed rehearsal instead.

Speed Rehearsal

Speed rehearsal is used by actors to rehearse and practise their script and scene. In their heads or out-loud they just talk through their lines as quickly as they can. So a 45 minute talk might take you 19 minutes with speed rehearsal, but it has a positive effect on you recalling what to say on the day.

Leverage your Preparation

I like leveraging – it's my goal for the next few years. I try to eke out some other benefit when performing talks. An example is my downtime when I'm preparing for a talk. Whilst practising or reading out the talk, have you thought about recording it to MP3 using your laptop, tablet or smartphone?

You can achieve a reasonable quality using the latest technology and don't need to splash out sums on microphones and software.

The MP3 can be used for a variety of purposes. Add it to your blog for downloading, send a link to the audience after the talk as a way to reinforce their learning. Generation Y will love this as they were born with earphones grafted to their heads.

And of course you can use it to help you remember the talk by playing it to yourself during your downtime. People have been known to go to sleep listening to the talk and swear that they remember every word subliminally. Clever, but I roll over and hurt my ears during my sleep, so I've never mastered this.

Memorise Your Talk Through a Journey

Do you ever travel the same journey time after time? A journey or a route which you know like the back of your hand, a short journey around your garden, through your house, a car route, a train trip.

If so, you're well on the way to memorising your talk effortlessly and presenting with no cards or prompts at all. Let me show you how.

First you need to put your talk onto index cards or A4 sheets and this must be represented by key points, and bullets of one or two words. Make sure the talk hangs together and you're not going to change it any further.

Now for each bullet that you've written, I want you to visually create something to represent the bullet. Something totally weird and visual, a 3 dimensional object is best. For example your bullet might say "USA comparison". So you put a picture of the Statue of Liberty in your head, but elaborate this image by putting a big beaming smile on her face, because the comparison figures you want to show the audience are very positive numbers.

Or you might have "Financial Services Authority" as a bullet point so you create a picture of Canary Wharf in London with little grey men in bowler hats emerging one by one, looking very sombre and officious.

Now the fun part begins. Start the route in your head and at every major point in the journey, place your object firmly so you can see it clearly. Put them in the right order of your speech.

Next run through your journey in your head and visualise every image you've created. There's nothing to stop you physically going on the journey and seeing the item, I often do this when I'm using the garden or the house as my route, but for longer journeys I use my imagination.

Here's an example from another 45 minute keynote on NLP in Sales, in picture format:

CHAT
K
YOU!
F
PH
WORDS
A
SES
IDEAS
HOO
FEEL
BOO

I've been known to place up to 35 items in my journey – each item represents a bullet point or a part of my talk, and because of the power of visual memory, I've been able to recall every single image. Try it, it works.

On the Day

The Slurp Technique

This one never fails, even in large conference rooms when you're presenting to hundreds of people. To drink water in the middle of your talk is as acceptable as breathing, so combine your drink with a quick glance at your notes placed carefully next to your bottle or glass of water.

It's that simple, I do it every time, even if I never glance at my notes. Sometimes just having your notes on hand is enough to calm your nerves.

Note Placement

Your notes can be surreptitiously placed around your presentation arena. I've been known to stick my notes to the back of a flipchart, on the floor if I'm on a stage as the audience can't see them, on post-it notes on the wall when training, next to my PowerPoint remote control, at the back of the room on a poster.

Slide Jogger

One of the most frustrating aspects of a talk is forgetting which slides are coming next when you have a mainly slide based presentation. For those of us who can't find the time, we create slides to help us remember. You know my views on this, however, slides do have their place in effective presentations. A tip here is to print out a handout version of your slides with

9 on each page, number them and keep this close to your notes so you can glance at the next slide before you reveal it.

That way you can correctly alert the audience to the next slide rather than clicking on the next slide, and glancing at it to remind you of what to say.

Dropbox

In case you lose your notes, ensure you've scanned or photographed them and download them to a service such as Dropbox.

Copy the public link to your smartphone so you can quickly download them from a convenient hotel PC and print them off before your presentation starts. Plan Bs are well recommended.

The trend of shoe gazing came to an abrupt end as the audience fought back. The band members just weren't engaging with their fans, so the practice had to stop.

Likewise try and prevent the onset of PowerPoint gazing by planning, practising and reminding yourself of your talk so you can free up your attention and concentration, thus ensuring your audience has an experience to remember.

The Great Q&A Dilemma

I was in China on business last year and discovered that one of their sporting passions is table tennis. I was amazed at how quick the players are batting the ball backwards and forwards without taking their eye off the game.

That's exactly how you should run a Q&A session. Here are lots of tips and ideas for doing so, in no particular order:

- However, a Q&A should follow an order. Never at the end, mostly just before the end so you can finish on your planned high. I've staggered my Q&As before when I've been speaking for a length of time. I've even allowed questions as we go, but only for small groups. Whatever you decide, let the audience know how you want to play it.
- Plan and prepare your Q&A. Naturally if you know your topic, then you should be able to answer most questions. Prepare the ten questions that if they were asked, would cause you to wobble. Research the answers, dig deeper for some variety in the answers and when they come up, which they will, you can answer them in various ways. Another advantage of this, which I've taken, is to put them on a slide and entitle then FAQs, in case you get no questions from the audience, and that embarrassing silence falls across the room.
- Occasionally I've written down some questions on index cards and given them out during coffee before my presentation. I've trusted the people to ask the questions, if no one else volunteers with the first

question. You'll find that once a few questions have been asked, others will organically follow.

- Keep your answers short and stop answering earlier than you normally would. These are not mini presentations. Move onto the next question. "Next question". Give the audience the gift of several questions, rather than one long winded one.
- If the questioner is dragging the question out: Many do, because they're in front of their peers and want to impress. With a smile state "Sir, can we have your question?" You'll get away with it if you smile.
- Likewise if the question is not a question, but is a statement of how brilliant they are, then just say "That's not a question. We can catch up on that over lunch. Next question please."
- Re-state the question. This helps others to hear it in the first place in a large room, but it also allows you to summarise the question to the core.
- Never ever say "That's a great question". Just don't do it. Not only is it irritating, but how much better must the next question be to beat that question. And the next one, and the one after that, they can't all be great questions. If you want to acknowledge the question, use "That's an interesting angle", "That's a fair question", or something like that.
- Do hang around afterwards to answer questions. "I'll be at the back afterwards or in the bar. If anyone wants to ask me any questions, I'll be happy to answer them."
- Maintain eye contact with the whole audience as you answer the question and return your gaze to the

questioner as you finish. Don't ask if that answers the question. Invariably you get a second question from the same person. This really irritates the audience, believe me. So invite your new friend to join you afterwards for a one on one. Instead just raise your eyes at them with a light tilt of the head to indicate that's your answer. "Next question please".

- If you don't know the answer, you could relay it to the group to answer or an individual. This can be a dangerous tactic especially if you do it with every question. There's always someone hooked up to Google, so swing it to them if it's googleable, and what question isn't these days? Better still, assert that you need to think that question through to give you a full considered answer and talk to them afterwards. You could have your email address on the final slide to enable them to photo it and come back to you afterwards.
- If you're part of a panel and I've been on several, you'll live or die by the ability of the moderator. The worst ones just ask every member of their panel an answer to every question. This is tedious and we start repeating each other. If you're able to, work with the moderator beforehand to ensure they know each of your expertise areas. If not, be brave enough to say "My answer was covered by Shelley on the panel".
- Instead of asking for questions in the normal manner, put a hashtag up early and encourage the audience to tweet questions as you go. At various intervals you can check for questions on your Twitter feed. People are more inclined to ask this way and it does give a use for the ubiquitous smartphone usage.

- I ran a session recently, ironically on presentation skills and we ran it purely as a Q&A. For 45 minutes as well. It was excitingly interactive. To allow it to swing along nicely I prepared a couple of dozen questions on index cards and when there was a lull in the questions, I walked up to an audience member and asked them to pick a card and read out the question. It worked exceptionally well.

Finally, try not to succumb to the "Expert Disease". This appears later in life when your expertise reaches such a level that you start to assume everyone else has a similar amount of knowledge. This is a mistake, so do dumb down your answers. It takes an expert to explain something complex in a simple way. It takes a dummy to explain something simple in a complex manner.

Getting Audience Participation

It was a cold, damp November weekend in London. The streets were bustling with tourists and people beginning to do their Christmas shopping. The puddles in the roads glistened with the Christmas lights. Inside a large hotel conference room I was sitting at the back of an audience of about 150 people. The celebrated speaker was going for it at the front of the room and doing a great job, I thought.

Thankfully I'd turned up early for this conference as I was speaking the next morning. I wanted to get to know my audience better and to get a feel for the theme and style of the meeting.

Luckily for me I did.

Over lunch I chatted to some of the delegates and I asked how the morning went. To my surprise, many didn't enjoy the session. "How come?" I asked totally surprised, as the chap was indeed an excellent speaker known throughout the world. "He just spoke at us…and didn't give us a chance to get involved and to do things," was the reply. "He was nonstop for 2 hours".

That was close.

That night in my hotel room, I completely reorganised my speech for the next morning to totally involve my audience every step of the way. If I hadn't done this…I would have bombed.

"Phew," I thought, "that was close". Ever since that day I carefully analyse every speaking audience so I can inject some planned involvement. Naturally, when training small groups we instinctively involve people every step of the way, but as soon as we stand up to speak rather than train, we drop into talk autopilot.

Surely audiences don't want to be involved, do they?

This is important. Some audiences just want to listen to you, take some notes and take action themselves. They want maximum content and lots of practical ideas around the subject. They want to maximise your time on the platform and get the most value they can. They don't want to be heard, they just want to listen. And you need to respect that.

This is the same whether you are addressing hundreds of people at a conference centre, or 8 people in the company boardroom.

Getting your audience involved is not always ideal:

It takes time, lots of time. My session, which I burned the midnight oil changing that night, was packed with participation and involvement exercises, but these took plenty of time to run and the amount of content I covered was much less than I had planned before I arrived at the venue.

You can lose control. Setting some form of exercise or involvement means you are no longer in control – your audience is. Letting go can be a hard thing to do for a speaker who has always had that control.

It's a whole different skill set to be able to involve and facilitate. Often the comfort blanket of what we know takes precedence and we snuggle back with our PowerPoint slides to get on with delivering information.

Why take the risk then?

But on saying all of this, why would we want to take a risk and involve our audience? Let's say they're "up for it" and you know some audience participation is needed. What benefits can it bring?

- Attention. Your audience's attention span increases the more they are asked to contribute. Just by doing this they can concentrate more. Body movement keeps people alert and has been proven to stimulate the brain.
- Learn by doing. People can embed the knowledge by using it. They can truly understand it when doing. Doing it gets it in the muscle.
- Alternative views. Hearing other people in the audience speak about the subject opens up an alternative insight.
- Personalising the content, for example through a question and answer session, makes the presentation more interesting for people.
- Show you care about them, not just yourself. This helps to build a rapport.
- Practise more skills. This helps you become a better all round speaker.
- Appeal to more audiences. My tailored presentation that Sunday morning helped me to appeal to this audience. It would have been doubtful I would have appealed to them with my original plan.
- More fun for you. Seeing people chatting and doing things makes it more worthwhile.
- Gives you time to take a breath and take stock of your notes and plans.
- You can carry on for longer than the standard 45 minutes. Involving the audience gives them a greater

attention span, so you can carry on for longer and give them more value.

I'm convinced, so how can you do this?

I'm going to share with you 25 ways to encourage audience participation. Some you've heard of before and some you've probably used already. There may be some new ideas you could use. To help you, I've categorised them into low involvement/low risk, medium involvement/medium risk and high involvement/high risk.

That way you can dip you toe in first to see how hot the bath water is.

Low Involvement and Low Risk

Audience Polling

Easily done to get a quick poll of the audience. "Hands up in the room all those that have..." or "Those people that think they are inclined to do this, could you please stand up" or "If you like that idea...cheer now".

Moving Amongst the Audience

With a roving microphone you can occasionally move into your audience just like Jerry Springer or Oprah Winfrey. Careful though, because you'll have your back to some people and lose eye contact, but it does break up the routine.

Tell Stories

These involve your audience's imagination, sense of humour and allow them to connect your world with theirs. This is subtle involvement.

Humour

Use humour where appropriate. Just having your audience laugh or chuckle involves them and gets those endorphins working, which injects motivation and energy into them.

Jobs for the Boys or Girls

Ask those keen ones to help with your handouts, be the timekeeper, or be the fetcher and carrier with, say, the roving microphone. It doesn't involve everyone, but it gets some people moving around, enjoying their role.

Ask Questions of the Audience

Easy to do in smaller groups, when training, for example. But in a group of 50 or more, this can be tricky as peer pressure may ensure you get a loud silence thrown back at you. Rhetorical questions are best earlier on. Also you could use this with humour. After a period of silence you could say...."That was a rhetorical question, by the way."

Put People's Names in Your Speech

Do a little research beforehand to find out who's who in the organisation. Who doesn't mind being mentioned and having their name used?

Medium Involvement and Medium Risk

Use Audience Questionnaires

Have your handout buddies distribute a short questionnaire connected to the subject and ask people to complete these. Keep them short and self explanatory, at least with the instructions on what to do printed on the sheet.

The last thing you want is people asking questions about how to fill it in. For example you could be talking about leadership styles and you could use a one page sheet with a few short questions which could show everyone their leadership style. Afterwards you could ask for a show of hands for this style and this style and so on. It's time consuming but really interactive. You could have a sheet put on every chair before your audience arrives to save time.

Partner Pledge

Quick and simple and ensures people start to take action following your input. Ask them to turn to a partner and make a pledge to them on what you're going to do when you leave today. Afterwards you could ask for one or two volunteers to say to the whole group what they're going to do. Ideally prime these people early on, that way you won't have an embarrassing silence.

Group Discussion

An old favourite in training circles and has its place in speaking as well. Set up a topic to be discussed which needs personal thoughts and ideas and then ask everyone to turn to their partner to discuss the topic for, say, 5 minutes. Alternatively ask two people sitting next to each other to join in with the two people in front of them, who could turn their chairs around. Or set up bistro style sitting arrangements where you automatically have small groups. Ask each group to appoint a spokesperson who will need to feed back to the whole room.

The trick is to get their attention back to you when the activity has finished. Bring people back to the room using the Thunderbirds theme on your laptop "5…4…3…2…1…we are go…Thunderbirds are go". Or you could simply say it with the accent and emphasis.

Use a claxon horn or a bell or something that will soon anchor the audience to know you want them back in the room. I saw someone doing an impersonation of the hypnotist from Little Britain the other day. Brilliant. "3,2,1…you're back in the room."

Questions From the Audience

As traditional as roast turkey on Christmas Day. Usually taken at the end of the presentation and that's fine as long as people know. You could take questions periodically, say, every 30 minutes. Or you could ask for them at any time and this is usually OK for smaller groups. But the worst scenario is that no one wants to ask a question. Faced with this prospect, you could dish out index cards to everyone and get them to write questions anonymously. Ask them to pass the completed cards around the audience and ask people to read these out. Since the question doesn't belong to them, you'll get lots of people volunteering.

A great idea I saw the other day with a young audience, was phone text messaging. The speaker asked everyone to text a question to her mobile number. Sure enough, within a few minutes the speaker was able to read out the questions she was receiving and answer them. Very clever and it appealed to the young audience.

Smartphones are beginning to take over along with wireless hotspots everywhere, so you could even get them to email their questions to your laptop.

Use Audience Photos

You need permission for this, but you could incorporate audience pictures into your PowerPoint presentation. I did this on that cold November weekend in London. On the Saturday afternoon I took pictures of people and asked them if I could include them in my presentation. They were only too pleased and it worked very well.

High Involvement and High Risk

Forum Theatre

This is great fun and allows audience members to get involved in a role play without actually role playing. Let me give you one example of how this works and there's plenty more. You need some actors on the stage or some very outgoing and enthusiastic audience members. Set up a situation, for example a sales scenario, and tell the actors, secretly, to do it badly. Run the acting for a few minutes and then ask the audience what they're doing badly and how they could do it differently. Ask the audience to give their ideas straight to the actors who then act out this way or using their words, or whatever was suggested. It's really involving.

Flipcharts Around the Room

Here you want some input from the audience in the form of ideas or suggestions linked to a subject. Have flipchart easels placed around the room beforehand and write on each chart the subject you want ideas on or the question to answer. Next put audience members into teams and ask them to physically walk over to a flipchart. You're pretty much dividing the audience amongst the charts here. Shout "go" and ask them to write down their ideas. After 2 minutes ask them to move onto the next chart and do the same thing. After about 10 minutes you should have lots of ideas or input to use how you wish.

Energisers

We know what these are, don't we? Activities that put energy into the group. There are thousands out there, some risky some not, but they all serve the purpose of re-energising the audience in some way. The best ones are where the actual energiser is connected to the subject in some way, otherwise some people think they're wasting their time.

Quizzes

Highly energetic and can be run in countless ways. Teams, individuals, it doesn't matter. The point is that you've prepared some questions on the topic and you're going to run a quiz of some description to teach further information or test to see what people have learnt in a fun manner. Easy when you have smaller groups, but large groups will work too. I've seen pub quizzes run with up to 70 or 80 people. Teams are needed here and more time should be given after each question for the teams to huddle and discuss the answer before they write it down.

Volunteers on the Stage

Does what it says on the tin. Let me give you an example to get you thinking about this. A speaker asked for 12 volunteers from the audience to come onto the stage and act out a particular character. The characters were all the challenging types of delegate you can get on training courses – the joker, the griper, the dinosaur, etc. I and 11 others volunteered and we had great fun acting out scenarios that were pre arranged by the speaker.

She had no problem getting 12 volunteers because the audience consisted of like minded people, but if you do this, you need to be certain you'll get volunteers coming up. You might get people on your side earlier on in the day so they already know they're going to volunteer. Remember to award these people with praise and applause. Little gifts or small toys are also a wonderful gesture from you.

Bistro Exercises

My final suggestion for you and the most effective. It is the bistro set up I used on that cold November Sunday. I had permission from the audience the day before to actively involve them throughout the presentation and I did. I arranged the room so that we had bistro tables which contained about a dozen people each. I then organised a series of games, activities, exercises that each table would do amongst themselves, facilitated by me.

For example we asked alternate tables to act out body language movements and the adjoining table had to guess what the body language meant. We had tables solving puzzles and riddles to learn more about the subject. We set various syndicate exercises for each table. Each exercise had the instructions on handouts or on PowerPoint slides so that the instructions were clear. All in all it was extremely interactive…but then again I had permission from my audience…will you?

So there we have 18 suggestions for you to involve your audiences, ranging from low involvement to high participation. Remember to check out your audience first before you encourage involvement and prepare well in advance. Some audiences really don't want to participate. Imagine the scene…you're sitting at the back of a large room expecting a content rich speaker just to give you lots of information and ideas. You just want to listen and take notes. And then you hear the dreaded words "And now for audience participation…"

Alternatively you could be sitting at the back of the room; the speaker has been talking nonstop for 45 minutes and you're tired, your legs are stiff, your mind begins to wander and you begin to think about your holiday lounging on that sun bed by the pool without a care in the world and suddenly… Zzzzzzzz.

Wrapping Up

Three Great Seminar Endings

How Difficult is it to Change?

This exercise can and does work with groups ranging from 6 to 600 and is an excellent way of driving home the point that changing is difficult. It is used to encourage seminar participants to take action and make some changes that will affect their lives. Many speakers use words to say this point, but this exercise proves the point with action.

Ask the group to pair off, male to male and female to female, and find some space around the floor. Once they are ready, and this can take some time, announce the instructions. With a very large audience, you may wish to put the instructions on a slide.

Ask them to choose 2 items of clothing or accessories and swap them with the other person. Initially people will be reticent, but most will soon get into the spirit.

Once the noise dies down, ask the group how difficult it was to change. Encourage feedback if you have a small enough group or announce the difficulties if you have a large group. People will all agree that changing is a challenge.

Make your point now that as a result of the seminar, you have been learning many things and it's important to take action and change the way you act or perform to ensure all the valuable things you've learnt are put into practice.

Now carefully ask them to take their seats again. You will notice that virtually everyone will re-exchange their items with the other person before they sit down.

When everyone is comfortable, ask them why they returned their items to the other person, since strictly speaking, you didn't ask them to do so. People will be a little embarrassed and now you should make the point that change can be done but it is very easy to go back to the way things always were. We must ensure that any change we make continues and becomes second nature, like wearing your own clothes.

A neat exercise that will take about 10 minutes depending on the size of your group.

Who Wants the Tenner

This is a very simple exercise that'll last a few minutes, if that, but has an incredible effect.

Towards the end of your seminar, hold up a £10 note (or fiver if it's close to pay-day). Ask the question carefully, "Who wants this tenner?" Your audience will all put up their hands politely and occasionally someone will walk up towards you and take it.

)ccasionally you have to encourage people to take it since it's ›lite not to, and most people are polite.

ce someone has taken the tenner, applaud this person as have taken action. Sometimes we literally have to get off ›ottoms and make the changes that will affect our lives. dy else will do it for you and results don't come on a Waiting and sitting doesn't always get you results.

›ccasionally colour photocopied a ten pound note and ks really well as most people can't see the detail.

However the person who grabs it will be a little cheesed off. By the way, it is illegal to photocopy money, so be careful!

The 7 Day Sprint

This is a slight variation on our traditional action planning that most of us do at the end of seminars but is rather clever.

Draw on a flipchart or whiteboard a box with 6 boxes within. Something like this:

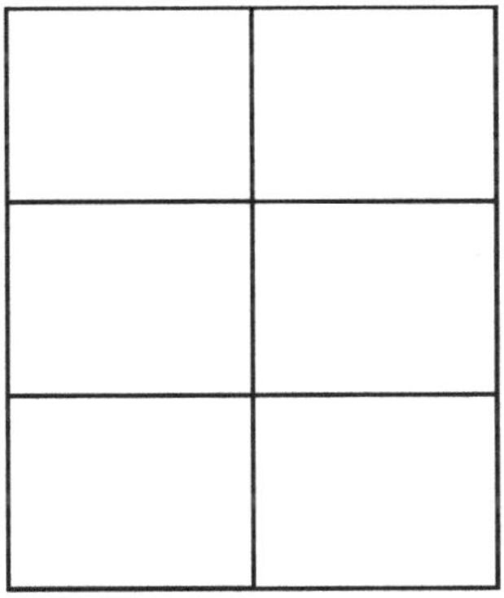

Ask the group to re-create this shape in their workbook or piece of paper. You are going to give them a 7 day sprint and they must complete each box during the next 7 days.

Now start putting the headings for each box. The headings can vary according to the programme you are running. For sales you might use:

- Prospecting
- Selling more
- Social
- Family

- Me
- Contact

As you write each one on the board, explain further what they need to write in the box. Prospecting here would mean that they need to write an idea in the box which will get them a new customer. Social would be one thing they're going to do socially. Family is one hour of quality time with the whole family. Me could be one thing that you're going to do personally. Contact could be one person they have lost touch with, to get back in contact. No regrets, just get back in contact.

Here's a finished example:

Prospecting	More Sales
Family	Contact
Me	Social

Further explain that they need to complete each box in a week i.e. 7 days. After the first week, they can change the headings if they wish, or continue with a fresh box.

People have all commented to me how motivational this has been for them. Encourage your group to do this and take it forward in their lives so they can benefit from positive action.

Finish with Aplomb

Second place to an exhilarating start is a finish that wraps up your presentation. Here are some suggestions:

- Finish with your main message, to ensure the audience gets it and knows what to do with it.
- Recap the major points, then call the audience to action. Something for them to achieve.
- Summarise with a story that neatly sums up the major learning points or message.
- Create a phrase that pays or a slogan to sum up.
- Ask a rhetorical question to stimulate the audience, then close.
- Use nested loops for any stories in your talk. A nested loop comes from NLP and involves beginning the story during the talk and finishing it off later on, in other words, looping it. You could leave the end or the punch line to the end of your talk.

I'm Paul Archer, I hope it's been useful. Bye.

DID2512913
L - #0086 - 080519 - C0 - 210/148/9 - PB - DID2512913